CREATIVE EVANGELISM

A

CREATIVE EVANGELISM

TOWARDS A NEW CHRISTIAN ENCOUNTER WITH AFRICA

by

HARRY SAWYERR

Professor of Theology, Fourah Bay College,
University of Sierra Leone.

LONDON
LUTTERWORTH PRESS

First published 1968

COPYRIGHT © 1968 LUTTERWORTH PRESS
4 BOUVERIE STREET, LONDON, E.C.4

This book has been published with the aid of a grant
from the Survey Application Trust.

LONDON
Lutterworth Press, 4 Bouverie Street, E.C.4

AUSTRALIA
J. H. Morgan, Lane Centre, 325 Flinders Lane, Melbourne
G. S. Cook, P.O. Box A351, Sydney South, N.S.W.

NEW ZEALAND
R. H. Horwood, 75 Kitchener Road, Milford 2, Auckland

CANADA
G. R. Welch Co. Ltd., 222 Evans Avenue, Toronto

CARIBBEAN
K. Jackson Marshall, P.O. Box 420, Barbados,
West Indies

FAR EAST
M. Graham Brash & Son, Prinsep House, 36c Prinsep Street,
Singapore 7
M. Graham Brash & Son, F-1, 12th floor, Mirador Mansions,
58 Nathan Road, Kowloon, Hong Kong

INDIA
Christian Literature Society, P.O. Box 501, Park Town, Madras;
Tract and Book Society, South Street, Bangalore; Wesley Press
and Publishing House, Mysore

SOUTH AFRICA
J. R. Dorman, P.O. Box 5532, Johannesburg

WEST AFRICA
Michael Sparrow, P.O. Box 3876, Accra, Ghana

ZAMBIA
United Society for Christian Literature, 3 Cairo Road,
Lusaka, and P.O. Box 274, Kitwe

7188 1329 4

Printed in Great Britain by
Billing & Sons Limited, Guildford and London

Biblical references are to the text of the
Revised Version except when stated
otherwise.

CONTENTS

		Page
Preface		9
1	SOME BASIC FACTORS OF THE AFRICAN SITUATION	13
2	EVANGELISTIC CONSIDERATIONS	33
3	SOUND DOCTRINAL TEACHING—I	66
4	SOUND DOCTRINAL TEACHING—II	92
5	A FRESH LITURGICAL APPROACH	118
Epilogue		156
Notes		159
Index		181

PREFACE

My INTEREST IN the fundamental issues involved in the task to make my fellow-Africans fully committed to Christ was first stimulated in 1959, when I competed for the Thomas Cochrane Prize Essay Competition for West Africa (French and English) and won the first prize. The subject of that essay was "How can the Church in Africa be both African and yet worldwide?" Of course, I had known all my life that many leading African Christians both in Sierra Leone and in other parts of the continent lived a life of religious pluralism embracing non-Christian practices. Such people were often devout members of their Churches but when they became subjected to anxiety and mental stress, they resorted to the diviner and the so-called witch-doctor. Most of us, if we would admit it, have been at one time or the other exposed to the risk of being drawn into that mesh. I had the good fortune of having been brought up by an Anglican priest as my father and a mother who lived a life of simple trust in God. They both individually and together led me into my first Encounter with God. When I was quite young they told me many times that I had been born four years after their marriage and, as far as they were concerned, as an answer to their prayers to God, for a child, preferably a son. So I was named in true African style, *Ebunolorun*, the Gift of God.

One experience stands out early in my life. When I was five years old we had to cross the River Sewa late at night not far from some rapids, and the boatman in midstream could not easily decipher the opposite banks, although they were not far off. I remember most vividly my father saying to my mother and myself, "Let us pray". I do not now recall whether he prayed aloud or not. Fortunately the light improved and we landed safely on the other side. But from that experience I learnt to call on God in moments of dire distress.

For the next decade, I was virtually separated from them because I had to go to school in Freetown; but whenever I was able to spend the school and, later, college vacations with them, I learnt increasingly that the only creative influence in life was God. Perhaps my intensive study of theology will not now allow me to subscribe to everything I then accepted. At the same time, I gratefully acknowledge my indebtedness to them for leading me to a real Encounter with God as a child. Their wide travels as Christian evangelists among the Mende, starting a few months after I was born, also gave me an opportunity of an encounter with my fellow-men, with Jesus Christ as the catalyst. As a result, I have learnt to cultivate a Sierra Leonean brotherhood which has transcended the barriers between Colony and Protectorate (now, Provincial) Sierra Leoneans. This sense of brotherhood, I value greatly. I myself have since come to discover that a true encounter with our fellow-men must be based on an Encounter with God.

Since the deaths of my parents I have come to discover a third facet of the life of Encounter with God. When at the Eucharist I say privately a *Memento Domine* for them I see their faces clearly and vividly. Strange to say, I find it hard to recall my mother's face at other times. But in the Presence of Christ I see her looking on me with a happy and joyous countenance.

For their role in pointing out to me these three aspects of the Encounter with God, I bless their memories. God grant them both sweet repose and the beatific vision!

In my older years, I have been sustained by the examples of both my parents to seek to understand how the Encounter with God demands total commitment and complete abandon to Him. In this search, I have (as a priest) found the celebration of the Holy Eucharist the opportunity of saying the only petition I now think worth making, i.e., "O God, do what you think is best". This petition, for which I have learnt not to try to know the answer, has been the most powerful mainstay of my life.

Readers must forgive this short personal testimony. But it illustrates my own experience of the three concentric circles of the Encounter with the God I serve, with God as the centre and the boundaries of a plane that embraces Jesus Christ and man—both living and dead. A real Encounter with God calls for a life of abandon. This is a painful sacrifice which all Christians must learn to make, and which they can make when sustained by the enabling power of God. Whilst, however, I make no personal claims of sanctity, I have been influenced by a personal experience of struggle and defeat, of pain and doubts, silhouetted against an inscrutable assurance of victory which I can attribute to God, and God alone.

My special thanks are due first, to the officers of the Survey Application Trust (World Dominion Press), for encouraging me to probe deeper into some of the topics I discussed in the Prize Essay. Second, I acknowledge a great debt to Professor K. O. Dike, then Principal of University College, Ibadan (later Vice-Chancellor of Ibadan University), and the Professor of Theology (now Canon D. W. Gundry, Chancellor of the Diocese of Leicester, England) for inviting me in 1961 to give a set of three lectures on some of the topics discussed in this book, and to preach the Congregation Sermon before the then University College. Canon David Anderson, Principal of Wycliffe Hall, Oxford, who was Principal of Immanuel College, Ibadan, at the time, also invited me to give one of those lectures to his staff and students. I cannot fully express my gratitude for the kindness and courtesy shown to me by these men, their colleagues and their respective students. Third, I must express my thanks to Miss Eleanor Macauley, the clerk to the Vice-Principal of Fourah Bay College, who typed the complete text more than once with considerable patience and remarkable accuracy.

I do, however, give pride of place to my wife, Edith, for her moral support in the thirty-one years of our marriage during which, for most of the time, I have lived in my study or in a library either at home in Sierra Leone, or abroad in the United Kingdom. In the last seven years she has contributed much to my understanding of the implications of an Encounter with God. Like most wives of University dons she has often been neglected. But Edith has found other avenues of creative activity —as a gardener, an officer of the Red Cross, and in various women's groups and coteries. These consuming interests have made it possible for me to spend my nights at my books when I should have been with her.

Lastly, I wish to express my grateful thanks to the Curator and staff of the British Museum for the help and courtesy which I have always enjoyed in that citadel of learned thought, and to the editorial staff of Lutterworth Press for the accuracy of the printed text.

The text of this work was substantially completed before the Consultation held from June 23 to 30, 1965, in Yaounde, Cameroons, on "The Evangelization of West Africa Today", under the auspices of the All Africa Conference of Churches. It is refreshing, therefore, to note that, in the Statement which was later published, topics like "the Christian doctrine of God", "the Creator", "the concept of sacrifice", "the fate of ancestors" (p. 4) and the "social solidarity generally found in traditional society" (p. 5) were specifically mentioned as requisites for a programme of Christian evangelism in Africa. We feel encouraged by the fact that contemporary concern for Christian evangelism in West Africa has come to realize the need for a fresh approach to some of the topics raised in the present work.

I sincerely hope that my readers will endure the many faults that pervade this book. If it provokes discussion and ultimately stimulates a greater mind than mine to work out a better statement, I shall feel that I have achieved a measure of my main aim.

In his Report on his first visit to the Rio Pongas, the part of his diocese in the Republic of Guinea, the Bishop of the Gambia, the Rt. Rev. Dr. T. Omotayo Olufosoye, writes: "What is necessary in this part of the world now is the interpretation of the Good News in relation to modern man's chief complaint—his encounter with 'meaninglessness'" (*The Gambia–Pongas Magazine*, April 1966, p. 13). God grant the Church in Africa fresh vision and new understanding to provide this need.

HARRY SAWYERR

Fourah Bay College, Sierra Leone.
Feast of the Epiphany, January 6, 1967

Chapter 1

SOME BASIC FACTORS
OF THE AFRICAN SITUATION

"THEOLOGY IN AFRICA has to interpret ... Christ in terms that are relevant and essential to African existence."

"A theologian who with the apostle Paul is prepared to become ... unto Africans as an African, must needs start with the fundamental facts of the African interpretation of existence and the universe."[1] So writes Dr Bengt Sundkler. Dr Sundkler seems to have had foreign Christian missionaries in mind when he wrote these great words, but they are equally applicable to African theologians and evangelists who seek to extend the Kingdom of God among their own people. Although space forbids us to examine all the implications of Bishop Sundkler's insight into the situation in Africa, we shall in the following pages attempt a synoptic consideration of the problems involved in adopting his approach, to which we fully subscribe.

I. THE AFRICAN INTERPRETATION OF EXISTENCE AND THE UNIVERSE

African peoples, except for a very few isolated cases, attribute the creation of the universe to God.[2] All existence is accordingly attributed to God. The implications of this belief are far-reaching. They amount to what we may call a metaphysic of Vitalism. This is generally formulated in the following hierarchy: God is the source of all life, human and non-human, and, as the Supreme Being, is the site of all power. He is therefore the fount and apex of all existence. Next in order comes man, who derives his life and power from God and is capable of producing life by procreation. He can also induce life and power into other elements of Creation. This is because he is God's vicegerent on earth. The rest of Creation is on a descending scale both of life and of power—trees and stones being at the bottom of the scale. The principle which is here enunciated is that all existent matter —human, animal, vegetable and mineral—possesses life, sometimes latent, but that any member on a higher scale can influence another which is inferior and make the potential power actual.[3] Ultimately, however, all power, all life and all existence derive from God and therefore belong to God.

This attitude is seen at its best in the relations of man to man. No one man is ever at liberty to take the life of another, or do him harm, because the other person belongs to God. If a man feels aggrieved and disposed to take revenge, he must first seek permission of God. So the Mende of Sierra Leone always invoke the Name of God before uttering a curse on anybody. Again, if anyone wishes to secure power to achieve some gain by accredited means, it is assumed that he has to use certain other elements of creation. But he, too, must seek permission of God before presuming to use any element of creation. As a result, one finds that everybody—the person who intends to use the most diabolic means of causing harm to another, as well as the man who is out to achieve success by the most honourable methods—sets about his plans by first invoking the "Permissive Will of God".[4] Thus it is universally accepted that every human being is under the protection of God. He is the ultimate defence which man may invoke.

The Mende of Sierra Leone, for example, appeal to God in the last resort when redress for a wrong sustained is no longer forthcoming.

They, like many others, also take an oath of innocence in the name of God, knowing fully that they are not speaking the truth and are, in fact, guilty of the alleged offence. They also know that those to whom one pleads innocence in the name of God are equally aware of the high probability of falsehood. But everybody tends to behave in the same way, because God is the ultimate protector of man akin to the Hebrew *go'el*.[5]   To those brought up in the context of Christian standards, and who have been taught to speak the truth always, this is strange behaviour. But behind an outrageous lie there is the deeper conviction that God does indeed know the truth; that every man belongs to Him, and that He is ready to offer protection to all who seek it; that although God does punish offenders, punishment by one's fellow-men can be brutal and severe. It therefore seems simple common-sense to invoke God's protection in order to escape the severity of human punishment. The lie told as a denial of an allegation is in fact a means of self-protection which the community respects.

This notion of God as man's protector extends over all kinds of action. When a man is successful in life it is thought among the Mende of Sierra Leone that God supports his activities by defending him from evil. So they say, "God is at his back". So, too, one escapes serious danger because God defends and protects one. Again, one commits a crime and is not caught because God is defending and protecting one. So the offended party is often heard to exclaim, "O God, come away from his back!" i.e., "O God, do not go on defending and protecting him!" When he is caught one hears the comment, "God has come away from his back", i.e., "God has ceased to defend and protect him". We may note here that protection is thought of as coming from behind the protected person, the stronger man as it were backing the weaker. This attitude is in keeping with the fact that when the Mende travel along the usual narrow footpaths in a forest they go in single file, the women and children going in front, and the men, usually with matchets in hand, bringing up the rear.

At the same time, God is said to punish sin. Margaret Field tells us that in Ghana "the divine attribute most valued . . . is the power to punish sin".[6] This is generally associated with the minor deities. But among the Mende of Sierra Leone, for example, when a poor person feels he can have no redress at the Native Courts, he usually says, "I invoke the wrath of God and the ancestors". The Sierra Leone Creole say, "God is never a debtor but he pays back (our just deserts)", meaning "God will (surely) requite a wrong-doer". It is significant that persons accused of a crime among the Mende never adopt a lie as a measure of self-protection when brought before cultic or other spirits assumed to reside in a "medicine". Similarly, lies are not tolerated when one is addressing the ancestors. The spirits are vengeful because they are regarded as akin to human beings. The ancestors, from experience during their lifetime, do not accommodate lies. Again, those who knowingly take a false oath on any "medicine" are later known to fall ill and have to confess the truth they had denied. Failure to confess the false statement may lead to death.

Because God created the universe and the elements, He is associated with the more powerful elements of nature—rain, lightning, thunder, rich harvests and fruitful seasons, famine and floods. But whirlpools, or powerful river torrents, are attributed to evil spirits because they always portend evil to man. Sometimes a person who is killed by lightning is said to have been punished for profaning God's sacredness, as for example among the Kikuyu, who believe that such a victim "must have dared to look upwards to see *Mwene-Nyaga* (i.e., God) stretching himself and cracking his joints in readiness for his active service to chase away or smash his enemies".[7] In other words, since man is number two in the power-hierarchy of existence, anything which is patently inimical to him cannot be thought of as originating directly from God. At the same time, everything with life or power must have emanated ultimately from Him. We might comment that, on the basis of the preceding argument, every aspect of nature is supposed to have an *ousia*, a basic *essentia* which may or may not be activated into a force.

Man, however, finds himself a victim of Nature. He climbs a palm-tree to collect the fruit. But he may lose his foothold and fall. When this happens, he may die or be crippled for life. Sometimes he encounters a dangerous snake in the tree and gets bitten severely. Or he may be hurt whilst felling a tree, either by the axe coming loose from its handle or by a falling branch. He may dig a large stone loose and be severely hurt as it falls away from where it was formerly embedded. A pregnant woman may be frightened by the sight of a chameleon: she concludes that the encounter with that strange-looking animal, with large rolling eyes, a large stomach and protruding ribs, is a symbol of death, or certainly of evil. The human male is puzzled by the fact that he hankers after a female who, at periodic intervals often associated with the moon, loses a considerable amount of blood—the life force of human existence— and yet does not die. She may suffer violent abdominal pains at this time but she also has the resilience which makes her recover within three or five days. Eclipses of the sun and moon are frightening, especially at the time of full moon, when a bright moonlight night suddenly turns pitch dark for (to him) no obvious reason. So primitive man postulates a demon which swallows up the moon and so causes the eclipse. Sudden deaths and incurable diseases puzzle primitive man; so he postulates witchcraft. These and other experiences lead the primitive African to the conclusion that there are other forces outside his natural, familiar sphere. In particular, floods, drought, famine, poisonous snakes, vicious beasts, diseases of all kinds, farm pests, destructive animals such as wild pigs or porcupines, all confront him with a never-ending struggle so that he feels compelled to create protective charms, or to devise other counter-measures which would send them away and give him a sense of security. Even within the context of regular human relations, he sometimes feels unsure of justice and fair play.

2. THE PROBLEM OF EVIL

As already stated, good and evil are attributed to God either directly through His actions or more frequently because He permits them. Nothing, however, happens by chance. Of the various manifestations of evil, sickness and death are most prominent. Among the Mende of Sierra Leone "health" is suggestive of God exercising aright His providential care over man and, by implication, He defaults when sickness sets in. So to the question, "How are you?" or "How stands your tone of

B

health?" the usual reply is "There is no fault (corrosion, rust) in (to be laid to the charge of) God", i.e., "I am quite well, thank you!" The Yoruba reply to the question, "How are you?" is "I thank God". God, as the strong One, bestows upon man good health. Sickness is, therefore, apparently due to a failure on God's part to maintain His power to preserve the health of the individual. But on closer examination the origin of sickness and death is only indirectly attributed to God. The Temne say that once God used to send down His messenger to recall man to Himself when he had fulfilled his allotted span of life. But one man who was rich, vigorous and wicked, resisted the messenger. God then sent other messengers whom the wicked man beat up. Two years afterwards, however, God sent sickness to soften him up. So he lay down and could not rise from his bed again. Later, God sent Death, who then took the man away.[8] The Mende of Sierra Leone talk of illness as "that which softens up an adult who is supposed to be full of vigour". In the Temne fable, Sickness is an old man but Death is a young man full of life and vigour.

Mrs Meyerowitz tells us that the Akan of Ghana, who hold their kings sacred, protected them from contacts with death and from contacts with a woman at the time of her menses because "it was feared that the loss of life-blood which is animated by the *kra* might be infectious".[9] A menstrual woman is supposed among the Akan to destroy the spirit which produces gold so she is not allowed near a gold-mine. Mende men believe they would die if they happened to be present at the birth of a child. The operative notion is that of loss of power by the king's vital energy, or of the power latent in gold, or of male energy through the influence of some other agency to which power is attributed. So the Mende of Sierra Leone and the Bantu of the Lower Congo say they are "dead" of hunger or of fatigue, or that the least obstacle or illness is "killing" them.[10] According to this type of reasoning, "Illness and death . . . result from some external agent who weakens us through his greater force".[11]

On the basis of a similar argument, a performing magician is very suspicious of others who come to watch his performances and takes precautions beforehand, by using appropriate charms, to protect himself from any hostile power which may inhibit his performance. Even professional stilt-walkers first arm themselves with adequate charms before appearing at a public performance.

This notion lies behind the belief in witchcraft—either in the form of poisons (the Kikuyu of Kenya), or the witch-cloak (the Kono of Sierra Leone), or the capacity of the soul (or one soul) (the Akan of Ghana) to leave the body whilst a person is asleep in order to harm the soul of a child or some other adult living near or far away. Except in the case of the witch-cloak, witchcraft represents the selfish desire to deprive another person of his power-force. Even in the case of the witch-cloak, it is supposed that the holder of a more powerful garment tends always to snatch a garment of inferior power from its owner. When this happens, the latter dies suddenly from a haemorrhage attributed to the wrenching of the strings of the garment from its owner's heart. The stronger power-force has diminished the inferior power-force of the weaker cloak and so death ensues.

Equally, the chameleon is supposed among some tribes to possess a force which in terms of destructiveness is greater than that of a child in the foetal stage. If, therefore, a pregnant woman encounters a chameleon on the road, it is believed that when the child is born it will develop the physical characteristics of that animal, i.e., a distended stomach and protruding ribs. A doctor might attribute this condition to improper feeding, but in the African situation the chameleon's power-force must be exorcized before the child can regain normal health.[12] It is also supposed that myriads of unnamed and unidentifiable evil spirits are capable of entering a pregnant woman, and tend to do so if she goes out at night. Being spirits, their power-force is stronger than that attributed to the chameleon and can therefore destroy the foetus. This is the explanation given of the birth of monsters. So pregnant women among the Yoruba and the Sierra Leone Creole, for example, either carry a pocket-knife with its blade open, or place several pebbles in their pockets when they go out at night. The knife apparently frightens the spirits. The stones are supposed to divert them from entering the woman's abdomen by counter-attraction, because it is believed that spirits love to inhabit stones.

Sometimes, evil is attributed to destiny. The role of destiny in the life of the individual is uniformly conceived, with slight local variations among the various groups, but the Yoruba attitude is perhaps representative. Dr. Idowu tells us that the Yoruba believe that before a child is born his soul kneels before God and requests certain things, i.e., he *chooses* his destiny. Of course, if his choice is reasonable, it will be granted to him. Or he may also kneel and *receive* his destiny. Sometimes, however, the destiny is *affixed* to him. This destiny, acquired in any one of these three ways, is to all intents and purposes believed to remain unaltered throughout the life of the individual. In this context a person may either have received or have affixed to him a bad destiny.[13] At the same time, provision seems to have been made for the alteration of an evil destiny to a good one through the good offices of a deity, *Orunmila*, who is supposed to be "present when man is created and his destiny sealed".[14] A votary of *Orunmila* can, therefore, invoke his aid to better his condition in life. On the other hand, it is believed that a good destiny may be altered for the worse (*a*) by "the evil powers of the world",[15] believed to be out-and-out diabolic,[16] or (*b*) by what Dr. Idowu calls the person's counterpart or *double*. This double, which is sometimes referred to by the Yoruba as one's guardian-angel, has to be kept "in a state of peaceful contentment through regular offerings",[17] or else it may become hostile to its physical counterpart.

The belief in the fixity of a man's destiny is closely associated with his head (*Ori*). One is born with a good or bad head, i.e., with good fortune or bad;[18] or with a quiet or a noisy head, i.e., liable to attract little or much attention to one's mistakes. The people of Benin also hold similar notions of destiny and attribute a man's success or failure in life to *Ehi*,[19] an equivalent of the Yoruba "double". The Mende idea of destiny is summarized in the proverb: "If you have been destined to eat your soup out of a basket, do not strive to eat it out of a bowl." The Sierra

Leone Creole say, "one who is destined to carry stones on his head must inevitably be a stone-carrying labourer". M. J. Fortes finds a similar notion among the Tallensi.[20]

To the ultimate question "Whence comes evil?" there is no philosophical answer. At the same time two possible answers seem to be available. First, evil like good comes from God, because ultimately evil spirits, the evil world forces, the potentially hostile *double* of a man, all derive their power from God.[21] Even sickness and death are the messengers of God. The most vicious man cannot hope for success without first seeking the permission of God and then invoking His aid for his diabolic intentions. Second, evil is thought of as the diminution of one's power-force. In the absence of any knowledge of physiology and of bacteria and viruses, man is supposed to be exposed to evil either through "attraction", as in the case of the chameleon disease among children, or through "association"—the risk of death when men come near a woman at the time of her monthly periods. In this context, death is the most probable evil. But misfortune in business—commerce, hunting, etc.—is often attributed to contact with a woman. So the Akan and the Mende used to keep young women off an army camp; the Kwotto hunter never allowed his wife to touch his hunting gear; the Akan kept the talking drums away from the reach of women.[22] A Temne farmer "must practise continence during the planting or reaping season". He must not touch his wife on the "night before a farm is cleared of bush or hoed".[23] A similar attitude is attributed to some of the tribes of Eastern Nigeria by P. Amaury Talbot.[24] There is a third variant, viz.: affliction by evil through "sympathy". On this basis, the Temne of Sierra Leone believe that when a man fails on a mission to some distant place, his wife has committed adultery in his absence. Evil seems to be due to the violation of world-order.

3. THE EARTH GODDESS

Because primitive man was largely dependent on the agricultural products he grew, his life became closely related to the factors affecting the soil and to the soil itself; various fertility cults were created to which the prosperity of the crops was attributed. So the Akan postulated both a Goddess of "fertility and procreation", *Asaase Afua*, and a Goddess of "the barren soil of Earth", and of "Death", *Asaase Yaa*, both Earth Goddesses, and also daughters of *Nyame*, the Great Lunar Goddess Mother. These two Goddesses have been combined as *Asaase Afua* in "Bono and some other Akan states", and as *Asaase Yaa* "in Asante". Writers on Akan religion differ as to whether *Asaase Yaa* is worshipped or not. Rattray and Mrs. Eva Meyerowitz say she is. Rattray has recorded prayers offered to *Asaase Yaa* when offerings are made at the annual tilling of the soil prior to sowing the seed.[25] Busia, on the other hand, denies this. He observes that "The Earth was regarded as possessing a spirit or power of its own which was helpful if propitiated, and harmful if neglected". Thursday is set apart as sacred in honour of *Asaase Yaa*, and no farming is to be undertaken on that day. So when in 1942 the Ashanti Confederacy Council decreed Thursday as a day of rest, because it was sacred to *Asaase Yaa*, Christians protested violently to the Government.[26]

The Ibo of Nigeria are also known to worship an Earth Goddess, *Ale* or *Ala*, who is said to be held in such high esteem that only the head chief of a town can aspire to be her priest.[27] The Mende of Sierra Leone also postulate what is tantamount to an Earth Goddess, *Maa Ndɔɔ*, (Grand) Mother Earth, sometimes referred to as *Maa Ŋgewɔ*, Mother God. So, too, the people of the Lower Congo believe in the existence of an earthly counterpart of their Supreme God, *Nzambi*, known also as *Nzambi*, who "lives in a huge termite" and "who during the rainy season . . . held back the rain because of the people's unrighteousness".[28] It is not clear if the Mende worship *Maa Ndɔɔ*. But some of the most sacred oaths begin with an invocation of *Maa Ŋgewɔ*.

The Yoruba have a practice which suggests that they regard the Earth certainly as a Power. Two men wishing to enter a covenant dig a hole in the ground, pour water into it, and, after splitting a kola-nut into two, cast the halves into the water.

They then kneel face to face with the hole between them and invoke the Earth to witness the covenant, each in turn sipping some of the water and eating a piece of the kola-nut. This rite Idowu calls "Drinking the Earth together", or "Drinking together from the Earth".[29] The Earth is thus seen to be regarded as an external agency, of greater potential than man's. In addition, the earth is associated with the dead ancestors, who are identified with the land in which they lie buried. Their physical bodies become mingled with the soil, and so they inevitably become part of it.

The reluctance found in some parts of Africa (e.g., West Africa) to part with land is based on the primary fact that until modern sanitation rules were enforced by the colonial powers, a man was buried in his house or in the grounds in which his hut is erected.[30] The same principle applies to the tribal cults. In Sierra Leone, for example, every *Poro Bush*, i.e., chapter, contains the grave of its founder. In the old days, Temne chiefs were buried in the *Poro Bush*. The sacred groves are sacred principally because they contain the graves of the national heroes. About twenty years ago, when a town in Sierra Leone was to be extended, the extension had to intrude upon one such sacred grove. The project was at first unpopular and so resisted by the elders. But, after feelings had died down, the graves in the grove were dug open and such of the remains of the heroes as could be removed were taken out and transferred to another site; only then could the grove be cut down.

Again, because the dead ancestors are supposed to be re-incarnated in their descendants in the case of old people, or in their successors in the case of babies, a popular version of *creationism* attributes the soul (or perhaps one of several souls) of babies to the earth. Thus among the Kroo of Liberia and Sierra Leone, before the first baby to die in a family is buried, he is restored to the ancestors represented by an old female member of the family. She addresses the ancestors after the child has been laid in the coffin, requesting that the child returns to his parents at the earliest opportunity.[31] Here the ancestors are in effect identified with Mother Earth. The child to be buried naturally goes to the earth, but will in fact be received by the ancestors. So, if and when he is to return to life, he must be restored to his parents both by Mother Earth and the ancestors in a combined operation. A similar consideration seems to be implied when the blood shed at circumcision is allowed to drop on the ground. Circumcision-blood unites the patient to the ancestors and at the same time brings his life (through this blood) into direct contact with Mother Earth.[32] The practice of pouring libations of water on the ground and of placing food in a hole (sometimes left un-covered) for the use of the ancestors implies a similar considera-tion.

We may, therefore, go on to suggest that Mother Earth is thought of first as a Creative Power. This aspect is seen most clearly in the growth of crops and the general flora. When the grasses die and large trees decay through old age they return to the earth, and form humus. More important than all these, since cremation is primarily employed as a punishment for sorcery and witchcraft, human beings, dear to their families and in some instances to the whole clan or tribe, are buried in the soil and return to the earth with all their capabilities. So the earth acquires another characteristic; it is the home of the dead and absorbs their vital powers. It receives and retains the dead in its womb. Thus it acquires the characteristics of a pregnant mother. The contrary proposition that children come from the earth is there-fore natural. Pregnancy leads to birth at some time. The Earth is thus endowed with the dual capacity both to absorb at death plants and men, and also to produce their replacements in fresh vegetable growths, as well as in the birth of children. The processes involved are, however, mysterious and constitute a *kratophony*. So she is worshipped as by some of the tribes of the Niger Delta.

Earth and Sky thus become two poles around which human existence revolves, each conceived as a Power; the Sky with its more terrifying peals of thunder, its fearsome lightnings and raging tempests, positively cowing man to submissiveness.[33] We can therefore understand why a sudden tropical thunderstorm is in some parts of Sierra Leone attributed to a gun-fight between owners of witches' cloaks—the lightning representing the flash of the explosion, and the thunder the consequential sound produced by gun-fire. Rain, sometimes in tropical cloud-bursts, also comes from the Sky. So among the Bantu rain is called by the name of the Sky-god, *Leza*. But the Sky is also traversed by the Sun which gives light and heat—a factor which makes plants grow—and by the Moon which provides a gentle light for travellers. So a Sky-god is postulated, and, as in Ghana, first the Moon and then the Sun become identified with Him. He is a Creator. But as among the Kikuyu, He can destroy the irreverent with lightning.

On the other hand, the bowels of the Earth are associated with darkness and with death. But it also produces life in a way even scientific man has not fully understood. It can also be barren—even though sometimes this condition is the result of over-cultivation. In any case, no crops grow in a barren tract of land and the people who live on it are apt to die for lack of food. So planting ceremonies are instituted to court the good-will of the Earth. Sexual intercourse during planting seasons is eschewed because this is a dispersal of "seed", at a time when all seed-energy should be concentrated in a single system. Illicit relations, especially in the fields or in the forest, pollute the land, perhaps because to spill "seed" indiscriminately on the ground might initiate a species of crops unrelated to the known forms of vegetable life. Of course, it may also have been felt that, where such marital relations resulted in pregnancy, the offspring might be abnormal—giants, dwarfs or monsters. One can therefore understand why harvest festivals are so important to the primitive African. In the old days a human life was offered in grateful return for a good yield of the crops. Mother Earth is accordingly endowed with the quality of a goddess. She is not generally worshipped; but neither is the Sun. In view of the further fact that the vegetable life on Mother Earth depends on rain, one can see how the Supreme God is brought into close relation with the Earth Goddess in terms of seminal fluid first moistening the woman's body and then bringing forth children. So the people of Lower Congo call her *Nzambi*, after the Sky-god, and the Mende regard her as the Sky-god, *Ŋgewɔ's*, wife. One may therefore postulate that Mother Earth is regarded as universal a Power as the Sky-god is.[34]

4. THE PRACTICE OF THE PRESENCE

Canon J. V. Taylor in his stimulating book, *Primal Vision*, makes the comment that "Africans believe that presence is the debt they owe to one another".[35] This recognition of a Presence is of course basic to the hierophanies primitive man seems to encounter.[36] It is this fact of Presence that has led to the belief in the continued existence of the ancestral spirits and in their influence on their descendants. Filial devotion leads man to believe that his parents even when dead have a deep concern for his well-being. This is true of all mankind, but, from our point of view, markedly important in the African situation. The basis of the practice of the Presence seems to lie in the clan-systems that are held within the primitive African communities, and which may be depicted in terms of a three-tiered hierarchy of relations embracing (1) the living, (2) the dead, and (3) the unborn.[37]

The presence of the dead is assumed and invoked when the life of the tribe is threatened with disaster. Thus, for example, the Temne of Sierra Leone invoke the aid of their renowned ancestors when the catch of fish falls below a certain expected minimum or, say, when there is a plague of mosquitoes. The same principle holds good in relation to the well-being of the family and of the individuals within it. It is because of the reality of their presence that the ancestral spirits have come to be the co-guardians of the *mores* of the family, the clan and the tribe. So two Yoruba men who have a dispute readily go to the grave of an ancestor and take oaths of innocency, each invoking his death, if he makes a false oath.[38]

The more operative manifestations of Presence are, as is to be expected, among the living members, particularly of the extended family. Every member of an extended family is expected to feel some concern for the rest. In truly primitive circles this means sharing one's food and one's possessions. But this is not all. The children born within the extended family are supposed to be regarded as children of all the adult members of that family. The Sierra Leone Creole state this notion in a very neat proverb, "One person may bear a child but he alone does not nurture him". Indeed, the members of the extended family were once expected to take a hand in the upbringing of all the children. The extended family went beyond the bounds of consanguinity to the neighbours, without any modification. As a result a child was subject to punishment at the hands of parents, relations and neighbours if he misbehaved in their presence or even to their knowledge. So significant was this attitude among the Creole, say, fifty years ago, that when adults within a family quarrelled, special care was taken to ensure that their children were never required to take sides. Indeed, even though women who had quarrelled ceased to be on speaking terms with each other they punished their children if the latter were known not to greet their opposite number, and more so if they were disrespectful to them. This recognition of the Presence of all who were either relations or neighbours contributed in the past to a great sense of *camaraderie*. It was scarcely possible to escape their ever-present watchful eye, looking for misconduct of one sort or another.

Another fact of the practice of Presence is seen in the old ways of approaching another person. If a boy was sent on an errand, he had to learn first to greet the person to whom he was sent, and then to give him the greetings of the sender before delivering his message. He did not merely deliver his message and take a reply back. We must here note that, as a corollary of this code of behaviour, younger members of a community learnt to respect and greet the older ones wherever they met them, whether on the roads or in houses. Failure to do this was regarded as a mark of bad manners. Again, because of the practice of Presence, the ordinary African family usually cooks a little more food than is required so as to be able to offer a meal to an un-expected visitor who happens to call at meal-time. Even when no extra food is available a visitor arriving at meal-times is always invited to join in the meals and is expected to accept the invitation.

Although, judging from the instances we have considered, the practice of the Presence seems to be primarily at the level of human society, nevertheless it forms the matrix of much of the religious thinking of the primitive African. This is seen clearly in regard to the attitude to the ancestral spirits. Because it is maintained that the ancestors are still present with their descendants, albeit in the spirit, food is either laid out for them at nights, e.g., by the Sierra Leone Creole, or offered by their graveside, e.g., by the Mende of Sierra Leone or the Yoruba of Nigeria.

Among several tribes in West Africa whenever a bottle of liquor is opened a few drops are spilled on the floor for the benefit of the ancestors. This is the basis of the religious rite known as libations. Here the ancestors are addressed and an alcoholic beverage (and water in some cases) is poured out on to the ground to satiate them. Among the Kroo of Liberia and Sierra Leone, when the first death of a child occurs in a family, the parents go through a rite, *Disɔŋ*, which includes their eating together by themselves in a closed room. The Presence of the ancestors is, however, assumed throughout the rite. In particular, when the couple are ready to take their meals—i.e., of rice—a few grains are tossed at right angles to their sides to the ancestors by both husband and wife before they start eating.[39] As already mentioned, this is the ground of hierophanies. It also explains the belief that power can be induced into inanimate objects through the spoken word, as, for example, is the case with *Shigidi* among the Yoruba. The basis of this power is, in fact, the *logos prophori-kos*, the "almighty" *word* that goes forth from a person and therefore represents him and his own native power. Thus blessing and cursing come to be thought of as psychic extensions of the individual, the latter having demonic associations. The word uttered seems to be regarded as being charged with the personality of the speaker, for or against the individual concerned. Again, the fact of Presence explains why it is impossible to lie when an oath is taken before a cultic or protective or patron spirit because the spirit is supposed to be around and must not be disrespected. The writer is reliably informed that in Temne Courts, before Islam had taken deep root, a defendant in court, as soon as the court had seated, always first paid homage to the goddess *Lat* or *Al-Lat*[40] and the Emperor of Ethiopia, before the case was opened. It is natural to conclude that in their assumed Presence, the defendant would speak the truth.

Presence also explains much of the attitude to God. Thus, when the Mende of Sierra Leone knowingly take a false oath in the name of God, and are let off by their fellows, an instance of a convention which everybody accepts, the fact of the Presence of God as an adjudicator is assumed whenever there is a quarrel between two persons. Although the idea that the Supreme God lives far away from men in the sky is universal in Africa, there does also exist a complementary belief that God intended mankind, symbolized in man and woman, to live at peace together; and whenever this peace is violated God comes down to heal the breach and in some cases to punish the wrong-doer as well. This notion is specifically expressed by the Mende story that God, after having gone away up into the sky, created two chickens and later gave them to the first man and woman, one each, saying, "Whenever you wish me to adjudicate between you two, call me back (with this animal—the chicken)".

More significant in this context is the notion that God is the Great Ancestor and, like the human ancestors, He is always present with man. So the Kono of Sierra Leone call Him *Yataa*, "He is the one you meet everywhere". The Temne title *Kurumasaba* probably means "The God whose image we are". Dr. Danquah interprets the Akan name of the Deity, *Onyame*, to mean "the God of Satisfaction" or of "Repletion". Thus God, for the African, is both the great Ancestor who, perhaps because of the range of human existence and their activities on earth, comes to be attributed with ubiquity and omniscience.[41] As great Ancestor he is also *go'el*. J. V. Taylor therefore misses the point when he talks of the "lost Presence of God",[42] because He is thought of as living in the sky. He has certainly left out all reference to the God who indeed is known as (*a*) having come back to speak to man, (*b*) their Great Ancestor, (*c*) He "whom you meet everywhere", beside being the "Great One, above and over all".[43]

5. SIN

African society, as has been already pointed out, is based on a clan relationship embracing the living, the dead and the unborn. This is in effect a covenant relationship. The various *rites de passage* testify to this notion. Therefore, like other covenant societies, e.g., in the supreme instance, Israel, the life of the individual is primarily thought of not in terms of a separate existence, but as a facet of the community. So the corporate solidarity of the family, the clan and the tribe becomes a fundamental factor of life. This aspect of the nature of tribal society explains what is so often described as the backwardness of tribal society, the individual having little or no opportunity to exercise his initiative. Whilst it is true that tribal man has to wait for group initiative before doing most things he should ordinarily undertake, the writer would also say that the advanced individualism of the West has lost that solidarity without which human society does not stand together. Indeed, this solidarity is "indispensable for the maintenance of ethical conduct and a common standard of behaviour since only when every member of a group knows what society requires of him, and fashions his life accordingly, is a universal norm possible".[44] We shall refer to this solidarity and the consequential universal norm as a *sensus communis*.

This *sensus communis* seems to us to play a very important role in regard to sin. Among the Mende of Sierra Leone, the *Poro* Society places a ban on the palm-fruit so that the fruit is not cut by those who might be inclined to gather more than their share, because most of the men would be engaged in preparing their farms for sowing, say, rice. If they violated the ban they would naturally come under the judgment of the *Poro*, and would be required both to pay a fine and to appease the spirit of the *Poro*. Again, when a Mende farmer set up a protective medicine in, say, a cassava plantation, he always allowed for a traveller journeying from far who might be genuinely hungry and there-fore might pluck a root of the crops to eat on the spot. The hungry traveller was thus allowed to do so without any adverse effect on his system. On the other hand, anyone who rooted up the crops to take home or to sell would be thought of as a thief and would fall ill.

Two features of the attitude of sin may here be mentioned: Among African peoples personal responsibility for one's actions is always to the fore. But usually this responsibility is extended to other members of the family. Thus, among the Mende, a man's sisters and brothers are required to perform rites of expiation when he offends his maternal uncle. Again, if the Mende wish to utter a curse in a case of theft, they invoke it upon the offender's father, mother, wife, children and even friends and associates, i.e., anyone who might have been privy to the act but would have been reluctant to report it. We would go on to state that the *sensus communis* assumes the role of a public conscience of which every member of the community is a part, and which he cannot in any way resist. So, even when his guilt is not detected by others, he contracts an illness which compels him to make a public admission followed by confession and a plea for forgiveness. We must add that the price for forgiveness often includes an act of penance, in the form of a fine or a castigation, or both.

Second, guilt is determined by *motive* and *intention*. Where these are to despoil the other man to one's own advantage, or where one is out to gain an unfair advantage over the rest of the community, sanctions are invoked. But these sanctions are not merely penal—catching the thief and putting him in stocks; they are regarded as offences against Society, and are given a religious aura. So the greedy man—who violates the *Poro* ban restricting uncontrolled collection of natural products, e.g. the palm-fruit —or the thief who roots up his fellow's crops, falls ill and has to go through a religious rite of appeasing certain spirits before he can recover. Society's anger at greed and theft is thus transmuted nto a religious idiom.

The same attitude is true of society's repugnance to incest, for example. The Kono prescribe public castigation of the offenders, ending up with their having to go naked, each—man and woman —to their separate bathing places, whilst being whipped. Offenders are required to run along two lines of men armed with whips.

The guilt incurred is now a sin, more so in the form of a *parabasis*—the violation of a law.

Basic to the after-effects of the crime is a deeply ingrained code in which the offender has received instruction often from early childhood. The offended spirit or deity is determined by a diviner, on whose priest the sick victim calls either in person or through his relations, and an appropriate sacrifice is prescribed. It is in this context that the general association of sin and sickness can be seen in its right perspective. Of course, sickness is easily attributed to withcraft; but if a diviner cannot diagnose witchcraft as the cause of illness the patient is asked to confess some crime he has committed. At the same time, provision is made for forgiveness by the use of rites of atonement related to the spirit which has been offended.

So, although sin is thought of as a violation of certain sanctions attributable to a cultic spirit, a protective spirit or a deity, in fact the essence of the sin lies in the violation of the solidarity of the community. So the society, in the interests of the preservation of its solidarity, provides opportunities for restoring offenders to the tribal family circle through prescribed propitiatory rites,[45] designed to appease the spirit or deity connected with the sanctions but also intended to bring the sinner back to the tribal fold. This cycle of violation of sanctions—illness–propitiatory rites–restoration—is of first-rate significance for our present study.

God does not enter directly into any discussion of sin among African peoples except perhaps in cases like the Kikuyu interpretation of a death by lightning.[46] On the other hand, if all the spirits are believed to derive their power ultimately from God, then sin as conceived in the African situation must inevitably be against God.

Chapter 2

EVANGELISTIC CONSIDERATIONS

C AN CHRISTIANITY TAKE deep root in Africa, clothed as it is at present in western garb and with little or no Africanness? This is the fundamental question that has to be faced if Christian evangelism is to make full impact on African converts. Enough has been said in the previous chapter to indicate the close relation between attitudes to life and religious thinking in Africa. It is, therefore, desirable to enquire whether Christianity cannot, as it has done in other cultures, borrow from the culture of African peoples. We recall the comment of H. S. Holland that "The Christian doctrine of God triumphed over heathen morality and heathen speculation neither by unreasoning protest nor by unreal compromise, but by taking up into itself all that was highest and truest in both".[1] At the same time, we would emphasize that the Christian religion emerged out of Judaism. In the language of the Epistle to the Hebrews, God had not only in divers manners and in different times spoken to man, but He had by a special revelation spoken also through the Hebrew prophets and finally through one who had the status of a son.

Whilst, therefore, we would advocate the assimilation of African religious thought-forms, in an attempt to make Christian converts accept the Gospel message and turn away from their pagan concepts and forms of worship, we recognize that they do not provide adequate material with which to express the basic Christian concepts. Indeed, it seems to us imperative to recognize the role of the major Hebrew and Jewish religious concepts as expressed chiefly in the Old Testament. Gentile Christianity without a Hebrew basis seems to us empty. Whilst Africans acknowledge God as Creator of the world, they do not

C .

explicitly acclaim Him as the one true and living God of the Hebrews, the God who speaks. Sometimes, however, as among the Mende of Sierra Leone, traditional customs are referred to as God's decrees, using the name, *Leve*. So *Leve* is said to have sent down the customary laws. We would maintain that the Old Testament represents an inevitable stage in the transition from natural religion to Christianity. We realize that some, like Roland Allen, think that Gentile converts must be provided with much Old Testament teaching before they can understand Christianity, on the grounds that St. Paul concentrated on such Gentiles as were already familiar with the Old Testament. At the same time, it seems to us that St. Paul was influenced in his preaching both by a thorough grasp of Old Testament ideas and by his experience of the risen Christ. An examination of 1 Thessalonians which, perhaps, provides us with the earliest teaching to a definitely recognizable Gentile community, supplemented by the account of St. Paul's visit to Thessalonica which we find in the Acts, seems to support our view. The evidence is as follows:

In Acts 17: 2, we read that St. Paul spent three Sabbaths[2] expounding to his hearers from the scriptures, i.e., the Old Testament, that "the Messiah ought to suffer and rise from the dead, and that this same person is Christ" whom he was declaring. Later, we are told that some of the Jews who had been aroused to stand up for the Jewish religion accused St. Paul and his fellow apostles, certainly Paul and Silas, of sedition—"doing what was contrary to the ordinances of Caesar, saying that there was another king, Jesus" (v. 7). Whatever may be the weight of the evidence available in these passages, we could safely say that St. Paul, as his custom was, taught that:

(*a*) Jesus Christ was the Messiah and so was king of those who accepted Him by faith.

(*b*) The Messiah had to die and rise again from the dead.

These affirmations, he claimed, were attestable from the Old Testament. When we turn to 1 Thessalonians, we are in not so ready-made territory for drawing inferences. But as we examine the epistle, we find sometimes that the apostle makes statements which imply previous knowledge. For example, the comments, "as you have received" (4: 1, cf. 2: 13), "you know" (4: 4), "as we commanded or charged" (4: 11), "as we said to you beforehand" (3: 4), "the word of the Lord" about resurrection (4: 15), "you have no need to be written to" (5: 1), "you know accurately" (5: 2). In other cases, he makes broad assertions which also imply previous knowledge, e.g., "The Jews put Jesus Christ to death" (2: 15); "God raised Him from the dead" (1: 10); "you turned from idols to serve the living and true God and to wait for His Son from heaven" (1: 9).

At other times, he refers to the use of speech (1: 5), "speech of flattery" (2: 5); "the word of God" (2: 13). On the basis of this kind of evidence we would venture to put forth an outline of the kind of instruction which St. Paul must have given the Thessalonian Christians. Some of our findings are naturally circumstantial, but the ideas are reflected in the more detailed discussion we find in Romans and 1 and 2 Corinthians. Others fit in with Archbishop Carrington's suggested *Primitive Christian Catechism*[3] as they are paralleled by passages found in the General Epistles. Our analysis points to three major concepts around which St. Paul wove the primitive Kerygma thus:

A. JESUS CHRIST

Jesus Christ is the Son of God (1: 10). He died for us (5: 10) according to the scriptures. The Jews put Him to death (2: 15). That act was a sign of unrighteousness and injustice. So they incurred the Wrath of God because this Wrath stands against all who work unrighteousness (2: 14 f.; cf. Rom. 1: 18). But Jesus Christ rose from the dead (4: 14). Indeed, God raised Him from the dead (1: 10). By His dying for us (5: 10), Jesus Christ has rescued us from the wrath to come (1: 10), as the prophets had foretold. The death of Jesus Christ symbolized God's love for mankind and teaches us to love one another (1: 3 f., 4: 9). Anyone who believes in Jesus Christ as his Saviour will be enabled by Him to abound in love to His fellow-Christians and towards all men (3: 12, cf. 5: 15). Jesus lived a life of holiness because He always tried to please God (cf. Rom. 15: 3). He will also strengthen your hearts that you yourselves may be blameless in holiness before God. In particular, avoid fornication and every form of evil. This is a commandment of Jesus Christ Himself. When you were heathen, you committed fornication readily; now, you are no longer heathen (cf. 1 Cor. 12: 2). Jesus Christ will come again; so be ready; consecrate your lives to His service and await His return (1: 10; 2: 19; 3: 13; 4: 17; 5: 2, 23; cf. 1 Cor. 6: 12–20). He will come as a thief in the night (5: 2); when He comes, He will judge all our work and the lives we have lived (4: 6; cf. 2 Cor. 5: 10; Rom. 14: 12). Because Jesus Christ rose from the dead, we shall also rise from the dead (1: 10, 4: 16, cf. 5: 10).

B. GOD

God is the Father of Jesus Christ and our Father (1: 3, 10). He is the living and true God (1: 9). He raised Jesus Christ from the dead (1: 10). The Gospel we preach demands faith in God (1: 8; 3: 7); it is the word not of man but of God who works in you to believe (2: 13, 5: 24); to reject our preaching then is to reject God (2: 15, 4: 8). To listen to God's call means to avoid uncleanness and to live a life of sanctification (3: 13, 4: 7). God speaks to us through His Holy Spirit (1: 5) whom He gives to those who listen to our preaching and believe in God (2: 13); indeed, His Holy Spirit works in them (2: 13). Those who refuse to acknowledge the Gospel and fail to believe in Jesus Christ, invoke upon themselves the wrath of God (2: 16; cf. Rom. 9: 32). Indeed, it is the worst form of sin to obstruct the proclamation of the Gospel (2: 16). God judges the hearts of men (2: 4); Christians should therefore strive to please Him (2: 4, 4: 1). To become a Christian is to answer the call of God for He calls us to His Kingdom and *glory* (1: 5, 2: 12).[4] Because God is living and true He bears (true) witness of what we do (2: 6, 10). He feels real concern for Christians (this is the will of God for us (4: 3), i.e., He has appointed us not unto wrath but unto adoption for salvation through Jesus Christ (5: 9)).

So turn away from idols, they are worthless (1 : 9, cf. 1 Cor.
8 : 4 f., 12 : 1 f.).

C. THE CHRISTIAN LIFE

Seek to please God (4 : 2); live a holy life (4 : 3); love one
another (3 : 12, 4 : 9) as we love you (3 : 12); work with your
hands, so that you may not be in need and will also be in a
position to win the respect of those who are not Christians
(4 : 11, 12). It is the will of God for Christians that they separate
themselves from fornication. So please take note (4 : 8, cf. 1 Cor.
6 : 17 f.). Do not return evil for evil but always do what is good
towards one another and towards all men. The Christian life
is full of difficulties and Christians must expect to suffer. This is
why we, as apostles of Jesus Christ, have suffered and have been
so badly treated and humiliated in Philippi and other places
(2 : 2). But we have been entrusted with the Gospel (2 : 4); so,
to persecute us is to resist God (2 : 15 f.). We have remained
constant; indeed, we have been emboldened by God to preach
the Gospel, in spite of any persecutions. We feel a special sense
of joy when we are called upon to suffer for the sake of the
Gospel, because Jesus Christ suffered for us who are His apostles
(1 : 4, 2 : 3 f., 2 : 15 f., 3 : 4). You also must be imitators of us,
ready to bear the consequences of becoming a Christian—i.e.,
to suffer (1 : 6 f., 2 : 5–12, 14, 3 : 7; cf. Mk. 8 : 34 ff.). Our suffering is the work of Satan, he who puts us through fiery trials
and tries to hinder our spiritual progress (3 : 5, cf. 2 : 18). But
God will give you His Holy Spirit to enable you to resist Satan
(2 : 13) and He will reward your constancy and faith with glory
(3 : 12, cf. 2. 2 : 14). (There is no specific reference to baptism in
the epistle, but if the evidence of Romans 6 and 1 Cor. 12 is
invoked, we may assume that St. Paul had taught the Thessalonians that the gift of the Holy Spirit is the result of baptism;[5] so
too are the inevitable suffering and persecution which attend the
Christian.) Pray always, celebrate the Eucharist. When you meet
to pray, some of you will receive special inspiration of the Holy
Spirit and they will prophesy (5 : 17–22). By your everyday life

and through your communal worship you will be able to build up the community of Christians (5: 11, cf. 1 Cor. 14: 12).

The reconstruction we have ventured in the preceding paragraphs is surprisingly instructive. St. Paul seems to have given a Christian instruction, using Old Testament concepts applied in a Christian context, e.g., Jesus Christ died according to the scriptures, but God raised Him from the dead. He gives us His Holy Spirit, who continues to work in us. Jesus Christ is Judge of all our actions and will come back soon to exercise His function as judge; but God is the final arbiter of our actions. God is Holy; therefore He requires holiness of His followers. God is love. Jesus Christ came to the world to manifest God's love for mankind. So Christians must learn to love one another. Jesus Christ did not requite evil for evil, so Christians must seek to do only what is good for their fellow-men; they must never requite evil with evil. The essence of Christian living is the building up (edification) of the community. Joy and thanksgiving must always be the criteria of such a community in spite of the inevitable threats of persecution and suffering. The latter is the work of Satan, the adversary of God and man. His implied references to the pagan religious ideas of the Thessalonians are directed to the specific condemnation of idolatry and, perhaps, promiscuity to which the term "fornication" could be applied; in particular, the sacred prostitution of the time, which was so prevalent in Corinth, and may have also been practised in Thessalonica, would be equally discredited by the blanket term "fornication".[6] Where, as in Africa, the pagan religious life may have included certain moral demands, this is all brushed aside and in its place the continuous influence of the Holy Spirit is emphasized in support of the new plea for holiness of living. If, as it is assumed, the "thanksgiving"[7] implies Christian worship and therefore the celebration of the Eucharist, then "sacrifice", *qua* sacrifice, is not condemned but, as perhaps in the case of the Church in Corinth, some attempt must have been made to substitute the Christian Eucharistic Sacrifice for the pagan rites.[8]

We may therefore deduce from St. Paul that the Christian evangelist in Africa must start on the basis of the primitive

Kerygma which embodies certain fundamental concepts, known only in the Old Testament, but adapting these to fit in closely with the more important new data based on the death and resurrection of Jesus Christ. Roland Allen has made the point that "St. Paul taught his converts to read the Old Testament and to read it in a mystic sense as applying to Gentile Christians".[9] Earlier he had said, "St. Paul accepted and delivered to his converts as an inspired book the Jewish Old Testament. With him began the strange process by which a book, originally the peculiar property of one people, was taken from them and made a foundation stone of the religion of another people, all its references to the original tribe being reinterpreted so as to be applicable to the new people, all its rites spiritualized so as to have a meaning and instruction for a people who did not observe them in the letter, until at last the new people so made the book their own that they denied to the original possessors any part or lot in it."[10]

We believe Roland Allen has overstated his case. The Epistle attests to the fact that St. Paul, himself a Jew, was struggling to express his faith in Jesus Christ in language that had become so current that his hearers did not need to have been familiar with the Old Testament to understand him. His own Old Testament training had provided him with such discipline as to lead him to a firm faith in the living and true God. He was thus able to base the new ideas on Old Testament teaching as a springboard.

Although we are today a long way from the days when St. Paul and other Christian missionaries first went abroad from Jerusalem to preach the Gospel of Jesus Christ, yet we are, perhaps more so now than ever, in need of such model lessons as we have seen in 1 Thessalonians. In this, the second half of the twentieth century, Africa, after many years of isolation from the rest of the world, and nearly two centuries of colonial rule, has emerged into a number of independent states of varying sizes, each egged on by a strong nationalism to assert new claims for things African. So we hear of the African Personality Cult, an appeal that we must all return to African Culture and revive the "old gods". This renaissance must be taken seriously. At the same time, there have, within the last fifty years, sprung up in the African setting various religious movements among the Christians; some of these have pentecostal leanings, others are an amalgam of indigenous religious attitudes with some aspects of orthodox Christianity; several of them practise divination; some, perhaps most of them, encourage polygamy, justifying their attitude with an appeal to Old Testament figures like Abraham and Jacob, David and Solomon; all of them have quite a strong puritan attitude to life, balanced off by an infusion of ritual, reminiscent of the pagan rites of the area, e.g., clapping, dancing, sometimes to the accompaniment of drums, prostrations, lustrations.[11] The appeal to the Old Testament by these dissident groups calls for closer examination. Let us therefore make a short survey of the situation.

In his then epoch-making book, *The Old Testament in the World Church*, Professor Godfrey Phillips presented to the missionary world a very detailed study of the circumstances associated with the study and use of the Old Testament in various parts of the world. In the chapter on Africa, he quotes a letter from one Mme. Coillard to her sister, part of which reads:

"I am often struck with astonishment when I hear F. reading to those people the Old Testament stories, at the resemblance between the manners of the Israelites and other primitive nations and the Basutos. Could you have watched their faces the other day as they listened to the story of Abraham, Eleazar, and Rebekah; every word seemed so telling; she, though so rich, at the well drawing water; indeed every detail comes home here with a force which dwellers in cities can never know."[12] Professor Phillips then goes on to aver that Africans of primitive tribes, extending over a wide range of the continent, seem to find the Old Testament easy to understand. Not only do the stories meet the human needs which Africans appreciate—food, shelter, clothing, concern for one's children, but also the stories are easily paralleled by local stories. Circumcision, sacrificial rites, and social customs like polygamy and levirate marriage, exist in the lives of African peoples. So too, divination, witchcraft and the cult of the dead are found in the Old Testament.[13]

Phillips, however, notes one specific defect, viz.: that "lack of a sense of perspective and of historical knowledge makes them find the prophets as obscure and difficult as do most Englishmen; and later books such as the Psalms, Job and Ecclesiastes are beyond them".[14] Earlier he had observed that "in both East and West Africa there are secessionist churches which encourage polygamy, insisting that it is permitted 'in the Bible'." Professor Phillips later examines the question how far the Old Testament should be used for instruction among African peoples and, if so, in what form. He comes down against the suggestion that because of the similarity which exists in the two series of myths existing in the Old Testament and the African corpus of stories, an attempt should first be made "to expound and appraise animism";[15] but he maintains that Christians ought "to communicate God's message, not the message of animism, in terms which are already understood".[16] To this end he proposed a short statement of a programme of instruction suited to the needs of primitive peoples.[17] Phillips wrote this important book in 1939 although it was only published in 1942.

More recently, Dr. Bengt Sundkler has raised the question again in his interesting and equally important book, *The Christian Ministry in Africa*. He points out that "theology in Africa has to interpret ... Christ in terms that are relevant and essential to African existence". Like Professor Phillips, he stresses the need for starting with "the fundamental facts of the African interpretation of existence and the universe".[18] Dr. Sundkler, however, goes one stage further than Professor Phillips by suggesting that the African myths "constitute an 'original revelation' which is re-enacted in annually recurrent festivals, in a rhythm which forms the cosmic framework of space and time".[19] He also refers to the similarities between the Hebrew stories and the African myths, with special reference to "the Beginning of Things" and "the clan community of the Living and the Dead". He notes that African preachers find the Old Testament a good source-book for most of their sermons. He then says, "the Old Testament in the African setting is not just a book of reference. It becomes a source of remembrance."[20] So the "stories of Genesis offer more to the African preacher and theologian than to the Westerner".[21]

These two authors deserve some attention in any serious discussion of the subject under review. True, Professor Phillips has devoted a whole book to the question of the use of the Old Testament among peoples ranging from Africa to India and China, whilst Dr. Sundkler has only devoted references to some aspects of the subject in a chapter in which he discusses the "Basis of a Theology for Africa".

But, by and large, Professor Phillips's work is more penetrating. He notes that a true perception of sin and its disastrous influence on man can only be found in the Old Testament. Indeed "the great Christian words such as 'sin', 'atonement', 'sacrifice', 'salvation'", or "the Christ" can only convey their full meaning to those who have realized how, in the distant past, "God led Israel through a long process of preparatory religious education".[22] Again, only in the Old Testament do we find the epithet "holy" applied to God. Referring to India, Professor Phillips says: "Psalm XV, describing who shall dwell in God's holy place, if assimilated in India would itself bring a purifying revolution to more than one form of religion."[23] We would add: For "India", read "Africa", and the argument will be as valid. Again, with reference to the support for polygamy which some Africans find in the Old Testament, Professor Phillips notes that (a) "there is no praise for polygamy, the stories frequently reflect the jealousies, disputes, and cruelties which the system encouraged", as for example in the case of Abraham and Hagar, Jacob and Esau, David and Solomon; (b) "the prophets do not have more than one wife, and throughout the prophetic teaching, there runs the suggestion that there is something better than polygamy".[24] So, too, with witchcraft, which is condemned (Ex. 22: 18; Deut. 18: 10 f.; Jer. 27: 9).

The Christian, on the other hand, should be taught of the omnipotence of a living God with whom man can hold communion. He should learn that God demands righteousness because He is holy; that rejection of these demands is sin and invokes God's wrath. But that through Christianity we are helped to understand that God is a God of love and that His love breeds forbearance which leads to His grace and forgiveness. Naturally, all this will only ring true if the convert to Christianity fully understands the Old Testament teaching about God.[25] He therefore comes to the firm conclusion that "the Church in Africa has much to gain from a clearer sight and firmer grasp of the Old Testament's true place and function in God's self-manifestation to the world".[26]

Dr. Sundkler, on the other hand, seems to shower too easy praise on the value of the "African stories" and the so-called "festivals of remembrance". In particular, it is difficult to understand what he means by the phrase "original revelation". How much more original are the African myths than the Hebrew parallels? It would be interesting to discover whether Dr. Sundkler equates the revelation of Yahweh to Israel, as the living God who speaks, with what he finds in the African stories. Granted both are revelations, is it not truer to say that the revelation which sees in God the guide of man's destiny; which recognizes that only He is Holy (cf. Is. 6, Lev. 17 ff.), which depicts sin as rebellion against God (Gen. 3), but which also discovers that salvation is of God alone (Is. 59: 15b f., 63: 12); which seeks to find an answer to suffering and provides us with the story of the suffering Servant of God; that this revelation, apart from the revelation in Christ, is the only one of the various other revelations we know of, which deserves to be called "original"? Dr. Sundkler rightly notes that clan-kinship is of great significance among African peoples, a factor to which Professor Phillips gives hardly any attention. But he has not discussed the importance of this clan-kinship in terms of the Hebrew covenant relationship—a relationship which explains the structure of the Hebrew community-sense.[27] We would say that the Hebrew clan-community, stemming from Yahweh, represents an original form of covenant relationship, one based not on pure human relationships, but, indeed created by God.

In spite of the criticisms we have offered, it must be stressed that these two authors have raised questions which are pertinent to the theme under discussion. In order, therefore, to arrive at a more systematic approach to the problem in front of us, we shall now proceed to examine in the light of the Old Testament the attitude of the African myths to the subject, "God and Creation", with a brief reference to Covenants.

GOD AND CREATION

As has been pointed out earlier, the African myths always postulate that God created the world and man in it but that He lives away from it—far from direct contact. The Bapedi, for example, say that God created the earth and afterwards drove spikes along the vault of the sky upon which He climbed out of the earth, pulling out the spikes he had used so that man might not be able to follow—perhaps to molest (?) Him. It is also assumed that God created the plants and other animals and either "the people" or a couple, i.e., a man and a woman. The Temne of Sierra Leone, for example, suppose that God created a couple and set them among the trees.[28] So, too, the Mende of Sierra Leone say that God created the world and stayed among the people whom He had created. He then offered to listen to their complaints, but as these became incessant He decided to move to some distant place where He could not be so freely molested. He therefore moved away to the sky one night, and next morning He was seen spread wide, far above and away from the reach of man. Again, the plants and other animals seem to have been created. The story refers to "the people" as well as to a couple. We are told that later God gave to the couple a chicken each, saying to them, "Whenever you need me to adjudicate between you two, use this chicken to call me back". So until today, as has been mentioned already, a Mende man or woman usually calls out, "O God, come down and let me [or, I will] give you your chicken!" when he wishes to utter an imprecatory curse against an offender. The Mende story represents an advance upon the other stories we have cited. It implies some communion between man and God, established by God Himself.

The Yoruba seem to be much more specific than any of the

three earlier groups already mentioned. According to Dr. Idowu's account of Yoruba cosmogony, the world was created by *Olodumare* within a series of creation activities. First, He created "the divinities" to be His agents or ministers through whom He was later to work, chief of whom was *Orisa-nla*. It seems that before the world, i.e., the solid earth, was created, there already existed a watery, marshy waste upon which the divinities used to gambol. Then *Olodumare* ordered *Orisa-nla*, the arch-divinity, to come down to create the solid earth. He gave him a leaf-packet of loose earth, probably in a snail's shell, a five-toed hen and a pigeon. *Orisa-nla* threw the loose earth on a suitable spot on the watery waste, and the hen and the pigeon set to work to scatter it about. This loose earth dried up the watery waste. Later, the chameleon, renowned for its delicate movement and its peculiar ability to look in two different directions simultaneously, was sent to inspect the solid earth which had been formed. He reported that enough solid earth had not been formed and the hen and the pigeon set to work once more. After a second visit, the chameleon reported that all was well. The creation of this solid earth was completed in four days. *Olodumare* then sent *Orisa-nla* back to the earth with a palm tree, the silk rubber tree, a white-wood tree and another tree called *Dodo* all of which were to be planted and allowed to propagate themselves. Meanwhile a group of other beings had been created by *Olodumare*.

They were sent down, it seems, from the "skyey heaven" after the chameleon's second report and formed the nucleus "of the human occupation of the earth". As the human population multiplied, they found that they did not have enough water so they appealed to *Olodumare*, who then sent rain on the earth.[29] No specific reference is made to the creation of animals, but they appear in stories associated with *Olodumare*. We may therefore assume that they were created by Him, perhaps before the solid earth was formed. The reference to a snail, a hen and a pigeon already existing in heaven supports such an inference.

This story is of unusual value because of the details it provides us. For our purposes, however, we may note, first, that *Olo-*

dumare did not create the world in the biblical sense. There was a watery marshy waste which, it seems, existed without the influence of *Olodumare*. Second, unlike the Christian notion of creation *ex nihilo*, *Olodumare* is said to have sent *Orisa-nla* down to the earth with some dry earth and a five-toed hen and pigeon who worked, presumably hard, to scatter the dry earth over the expanse of the world to produce the dry patches on which man may live later on. Third, it seems that certain archetypal human beings had been created beforehand, who were living perhaps in the heavens and who later came down to settle in the world and so founded the human race. Future generations of men were moulded from "the dust of the earth" by *Orisa-nla* although they came to life after *Olodumare* had given the life-less forms breath.[30] Even the plants and animals referred to in the story seem to have been pre-existent. Fourth, creation as described, i.e., the preparation of the watery waste for human settlement, was not done by *Olodumare* Himself but by His agents. The whole story is suggestive of the Platonic demiurge whom we read of in the *Timaeus*.

Wherever creation myths are found in Africa, man is said to have been created by God. But, as a rule, little detail is given about the creative process. Among the Yoruba, however, we are fortunate to have some detail. According to Dr. Idowu, there seem to be two complementary data found in the Yoruba myths. First, there is the notion that *Olodumare* created some pre-existent animals and plants. Second, that although *Orisa-nla* was ordered by *Olodumare* to mould the physical forms of human beings out of clay, yet it was *Olodumare* himself who gave them life.[31] *Orisa-nla* is, of course, thought of by the Yoruba as "the image and symbol of *Olodumare* on earth". He has been given "the prerogative to create as he chooses, so that he makes man of shapely or deformed features". Accordingly, "the hunchback, the cripple, the albino, are regarded to be special marks of his prerogative, either signifying his displeasure at the breach of some *tabu*, or to show that he could do as he likes".[32] Fela Sowande reproduces an *Odu* which gives another version of Creation, closely similar to the account in Genesis 1. The Earth was "dark and one vast mass of water and sky with chaos every-where"; "the Great Spirit *Ela* impersonated by *Eji-Ogbe*" commanded "that there be Light, and there was light; he commanded the Water to divide into two, for one part to go upwards, and the other to go downwards, and that the sky become visible; he also commanded the water on the ground to let the dry land appear; when the dry land appeared, grass began to grow, and all kinds of animals began to make their appearances according to the commands of *Eji-Ogbe*".[33]

He also quotes (in an English translation) from a Yoruba text written by Chief Fagbemi Ajanaku, the statement that *Olodumare* had ordered *Ajalamo* to mould man and *Ela* to supervise *Ajalamo's* work. *Ela* was later ordered to "go down to Earth to put things in order". This he successfully accomplished as described in the preceding paragraph. *Ela* was later incarnated as *Orunmila* and then "taught mankind to divine using sixteen ivory counters". Sowande adds: "*Ela* ... is the Life-giving 'Sun' ... Who as *Ela Orunmila* is both 'God' and 'Man', the major Prophet of the System, its Saviour and its Root, its only direct link with the Holy Trinity, *Olorun–Eleda–Olodumare*. . . ." He also mentions sixteen *Irunmoles* (the "Hierarchy of Heavenly Spirits"),[34] who "came to Earth" as human beings. These *Irunmoles* were part of *Ela's entourage* when he first came down to Earth as Spirit; they also formed "part of *Orunmila's* followers at each incarnation" (*Ela* was incarnated six times as *Orunmila*). To the reader of *Ifa*, these *Irunmoles* could be classified as the yeomen of *Olodumare* serving under *Ela* as their superior officer.

For our purposes, the two versions, Dr. Idowu's and Fela Sowande's, in spite of the difference in their content, pose the same problem to the Christian theologian who is looking for a *point d'appui* for Christian Evangelism.[35] Certainly, man was not, according to the Yoruba, created in the "image" and "likeness" of God. There is something fortuitous about him, or, in some cases, vengeful. The specific comment that God saw the created world and "Behold, it was good", to be later filled out by the comment "it was very good" (Gen. 1:31) is nowhere noticeable in the Yoruba myths. Third, the Hebrew conception of God is crystallized in the comment that He is a living God who speaks to man directly in order to reveal His Will.

This is the basis of the prophetic utterances which begin, "Thus saith the Lord". God is said to have spoken with Moses "face to face as a man speaks to his friend" (Ex. 33: 11). In Gen. 12: 1, God spoke to Abram and called him out of his home country. This notion of God as a living God who speaks is basic both in the priestly account of Creation and in the Yahwist description of God's dealings with Adam from his creation to the Fall, and with Cain (Gen. 4). The African myths might be said to present God, as both living and speaking, but with a fundamental difference. The Temne story suggesting that God sent messengers to humankind implies that whatever conversation he had was not with mankind but with other spiritual agencies. A similar situation is noticeable in the Yoruba portrait of creation, when *Olodumare* conferred with *Orisa-nla* according to Dr. Idowu, or instructed *Ela*, according to Fela Sowande. The (to us) effective speakers to man are, for the Yoruba, the divinities, the ministers of *Olodumare*. Accordingly, the *Ifa*-Oracle of Nigeria is associated with *Orunmila*, who, according to Dr. Idowu, "is said to be a linguist and to understand every language spoken on earth".[36]

Mention has already been made of the fact that the African myths struggle with the problem of sickness and death; of pain and disaster—of evil, *par excellence*, with special emphasis on sickness and death.[37] Death comes as a punishment for disobedience of the command of God preceded by sickness as a softening agency as among the Temne. But this is not of cosmic significance. Again, although among the Yoruba a woman with dirty hands touched the "unsoiled face of heaven" and so God, i.e., heaven, went away out of man's reach, no further consequences are mentioned. Among the Akan, God used to be near the earth, but an old woman, pounding her food in mortars, used too long pestles which used to hit God's body. He then moved farther away in self-protection; but the pestles continued to give him physical discomfort. So He ultimately went where we now see the skyey heaven. The story ends on this note.

The *Kposso* say that the High God *Uwoluwu*, when he wanted to create diseases, spoke to a man, *Sropa* by name, telling him not to go near fire, as that action would breed disease. *Sropa* disobeyed and so leprosy broke out on his body. But the direct cause of the leprosy was a bird *Ikono* which came out of the fire and beat *Sropa* with its wings. Death is due to disobedience of the High God's command, but never seems to be the result of His direct *fiat*, in the African myths.[38] *Olodumare* may be called Creator by the Yoruba but not in the sense of the Genesis accounts of Creation. No doubt He is wholly Other, and unique in status. He is said to be not just one among many, viz.: the divinities whom the Yoruba worship; "His status is absolute".[39] He is head over all and it is believed that there are perhaps 1,700 divinities who pay Him tribute. At the same time we do not find any specific reference to him as "the Holy". Instead, the concept "holy" is more truly attributed to "some of the divinities, particularly *Jakuta*, the thunder divinity, and *Sopona*, the smallpox divinity". Of course, Dr. Idowu says, "there is no doubt however, that the Yoruba think of Him as both ritually clean and ethically holy";[40] but he also tells us that "what can be gathered about the holiness of *Olodumare* is only by inference".[41]

The Yoruba seem to hold the view that *Olodumare* has been responsible for the establishment of man upon the earth and that *Ile-Ife* in Western Nigeria, about fifty-two miles east of Ibadan, was the first spot created (i.e., made habitable for men). This town the Yoruba claim to be the cradle of their civilization; in that sense, *Olodumare* is a God of history. Sowande has suggested, again making his deduction from an *Odu*, *Ogbe-Fun*, that *Ile-Ife* may be "a generic term for wherever a new beginning has had to be made on Earth, after one of the major cataclysms mentioned in History"; he adds, "It may well be that our present *Ile-Ife* was founded several thousand years after *Ile-Ife Oyelagbo*", the *Ile-Ife* referred to in the *Odu*. This town was destroyed according to the *Odu* after a series of "long drawn out battles in which huge forces of Darkness and of Light were locked in combat".[42]

D

For the Hebrews, the events of time have not been a mere repetition of the past. The Hebrew conception of history was inextricably bound up with the belief that God was doing something—which affected their whole life, and that this something was not a mere repetition of the past: there was always something new taking place at specific times with new effects on both themselves and the other nations surrounding them. Thus the Passover implied not only the slaying of the first-born of man and beast in Egypt but also the deliverance of the Hebrews from bondage in Egypt. The Crossing of the Red Sea equally signified the safety of the escaping Hebrews from the pursuing Egyptian host, and also their unexpected delivery from total destruction. Indeed, history to the Jews can be described in terms of God's *kairoi*, i.e., set periods of time, when something happened which made a difference to the Hebrews and which they always attributed to God as the One God. The African myths, on the other hand, associate contemporary events with an archetype which took place *in illo tempore*.[43] In a later interpretation of their history, the Hebrews attributed even the obstinacy of Pharaoh to yield to Moses' request for their release from slavery to the action of Yahweh (cf. Rom. 9: 17). For the Hebrew, perhaps the most significant criterion of God is therefore that He is the God of Miracle, who comes in to the help of His devotees in times of emergency. So, in fact, He is the God who comes near to them and acts in their favour. He is therefore a present help in time of trouble. He operates always as in the *present*. But this is of His own initiative. So He is known as the God of Grace. Of course He is also afar off and so we find a paradoxical attitude among the Hebrews which is not readily found among African peoples. Like *Olodumare*, He created the world, but, unlike *Olodumare*, He created the world without any form of material substance (Gen. 2: 46).

Whilst the Yoruba believe that man developed out of pre-existent beings, the Hebrews regarded the intervention of supernatural beings on human procreation as a disaster on the race (Gen. 6: 1-8). Of course, Yahweh is recognized in the thunder, in the earthquake and in volcanic eruptions. So He is like a consuming fire (Deut. 4: 24). He is wholly Other (Hos. 11: 9), and He is holy *in se*. This is, first, an aspect of His wholly Otherness. This understanding of the nature of God is seen in their attitude in the wilderness of Sinai. The people must not touch Mt. Sinai. If they did they would be put to death (Ex. 19: 9–14). The, to us, fatal story of Uzzah who died as a result of his effort to save the ark of God falling to the ground is another example. This attitude underwent some modification, as may be seen in the story of Isaiah's vision. The prophet sees the cherubim around the throne of God, each equipped with six wings with which they covered themselves, calling each to the other and saying, "Holy, holy, holy is the Lord of hosts . . ." (Is. 6: 1–3).

This wholly Otherness is, however, associated with God's omnipotence, which manifests itself in two other special ways. First, in the idea that Yahweh is a God of glory (Is. 6: 3). He is a God of "radiant power" who is in a class all by Himself. Man must therefore fall down and worship Him (cf. Is. 6: 5). So, for him to try to compare himself with God is a deadly sin. Second, God is a covenant-making God. As a result of all their diverse experiences they had come to realize that Yahweh was a moral God, whose word was always *Yes*, and *Amen*; that is to say, He proved reliable at all times. His special relationship with Israel was based on certain promises by which He had pledged Himself to abide, if Israel would serve Him. This is specially seen in the Covenant of Sinai which brought the various tribes accompanying Moses together and welded them into a homo-geneity into which later tribes were fused.[44] Indeed, as we study the social structure of Israel, we find that the Covenant of Sinai proved to be, first, the basis of their relationship with Yahweh and, later, the basis of the mutual relationships between the various tribes. So deeply ingrained was the idea that God never departed from His promises that it was rightly assumed that it was as sacred as an oath (cf. Hebrews 6: 17 f.). So after the Israelites had entered into a covenant with the inhabitants of Gibeon, Joshua would not depart from it when it was known that they had played a false trick (Joshua 9). Here, then, is another aspect of Hebrew religion which does not exist among Africans.

Significantly enough, African tribesmen live on a covenant relationship. The clan is held together by various forms of covenant relationships chief of which is that built around the puberty *rites de passage*. Indeed, Dr. Idowu has suggested that the Yoruba funeral rites are essentially "entering into a covenant with the deceased".[45] Elsewhere he makes the point that, besides various definitely ritualistic forms of covenant-making, "it is believed that to be trusted by a friend, to be bosom friends, to eat together or to be received hospitably as a guest, is to enter into a covenant which involves moral obligations. A covenant between two parties, means, negatively, that they must think or do no evil against each other's body or estate, and positively, that they must co-operate in active good deeds towards each other in every way".[46] In this context, the blood-covenant entered into by two voluntary persons or groups of persons is the classic example.[47]

However important the various covenant relations are in Africa, nowhere are they associated with the initial action of the Supreme God as in the case of the Hebrews, among whom four covenants may easily be distinguished, viz.: the covenant of the rainbow (Noah), the covenant of circumcision (Abraham), the covenant of Sinai (Moses) and the covenant with David (2 Sam. 7: 12 ff.). So vital is the covenant in the religious thought of the Hebrews that later on we find Jeremiah talking about a new covenant written in the hearts of men (31: 31–34) and Deutero-Isaiah of a covenant of the spirit (59: 21). Indeed, Israel as a nation was to become "a covenant to the peoples, for a light to the Gentiles" (Is. 42: 6). For Israel, a covenant was a διαθήκη based on God's initiative; in Africa, a covenant is a συνθήκη—an agreement in which the human parties played an equal part.

As a corollary to the above, we may note that whilst Africans generally postulate an Earth Goddess, presumed to be God's consort, a female deity was never acknowledged by the Hebrews. So significant is this factor in any attempt to understand the fundamental issues of Hebrew religion that James Barr has suggested that the Hebrews found the *Asherah* more offensive than the *massebah* because of their rejection of a female goddess.[48]

It is also significant that whilst, in the African religious fertility cults, the serpent is the prominent phallic symbol, in the book of Genesis, the serpent is represented as provoking man to sin and therefore invoking upon itself a curse involving total permanent hostility between it and man, with the victory on man's side. We may add that Hosea settled once for all the conflict between those who were prone to admit the Canaanite nature gods when he said that Israel did not know that God "gave her corn, and wine, and oil, and multiplied her silver and gold, which they prepared for Baal" (Hos. 2: 8).

Another related feature in many African communities is the assumption that the king is a divine ruler. The following instances are illustrative.

(i) Among the Akan, the chief was called *Nana*.[49] Since, in the early days, an Elder Woman ruled as queen, the early *Nana* was the woman who could claim that she had brought forth an *obosom* (pl. *abosom*), a spiritual deity, through the influence of *Onyame*. She was therefore regarded as divine because she had come to possess the *Kra* of the supreme goddess.[50] With the introduction of the Sun Cult, and the displacement of the queen by a king, the latter too was regarded as divine, and the incarnation of the solar *kra*. According to Mrs. Meyerowitz, the king received this solar *kra* from his predecessors in a special rite.[51] Thus the king came to be endowed with sacrosanctity, as the representative of *Nyankopon* whom he impersonates on earth. He "was venerated as the fount of everything", and was thought to give life to everything. So the Asantehene is reported to have said, "I am the centre of this world round which everything revolves"; it has also been said of him, "Everything comes out of him, he is holding the source of power, force and generation".[52] He therefore had to be kept free from all defilements; so he seldom left his place and when he did so his people "were not allowed to see him, lest their evil wishes might injure his *kra*".[53]

(ii) Among the Yoruba, the *Oni* of *Ife* is regarded as a divine ruler, in priestly succession to *Oduduwa* "whom the Yoruba believe to be their original ancestor and the first priest-king of *Ile-Ife*".[54] This *Oduduwa* is said to have been a powerful leader under whom some of the Yoruba tribes migrated into Nigeria.[55] He was later deified[56] and there developed around his name the legend that he supplanted *Orisa-nla* and had created the solid earth.[57] The *Oni* is in fact the 401st divinity of the Yoruba, on the basis of a conservative estimate of the gods of their pantheon.[58]

(iii) It is said that among the Temne of Sierra Leone, when a paramount chief dies, his head is removed and placed in the throne on which his successor should sit. By a special rite, kept closely secret among the elders, the new king is installed on his throne, and, it seems to be assumed, he thus appropriates the wisdom and experience of all his predecessors. The practice is strongly reminiscent of the Akan practice described earlier. By preserving the head of a predecessor king within the official seat of his successor, the whole line of the succession is kept in direct touch with the reigning king. As a result, a Temne chief cannot be installed whilst his predecessor is still alive. A Temne chief, therefore, cannot be deposed.

One might go on to say, that, common to the Akan, the Yoruba and the Temne is a tradition of divine priest-kings, established on the theory that the first priest-king was of divine origin, and probably deified after his death, as was the case of *Oduduwa*, and the Akan *Opanyim* raised to the status of *Nana* at his death.[59] We are of the opinion that this is the basis of *Ancestor Worship*. Once the practice of deifying the kings was introduced, the transition towards according godhood to ordinary members of one's family was easy. Among the Kwotto, we find that the ancestral priest-kings are invoked to pray to God for rain or other forms of national disasters, whilst the ordinary ancestors are invoked to give good harvests, strength to the men, and children to the women.[60]

The Hebrews, on the other hand, did not deify their dead. The mourning rites practised by the surrounding tribes were prohibited in Israel (Lev. 19: 28, Deut. 14: 1), because the Israelites held themselves to be in a special relationship to Yahweh; they were sons of Yahweh (Deut. 14: 2). Hebrew literature represented the dead as subsisting in a tenuous, shadowy existence in Sheol (cf. Is. 14: 10 ff.), although they could sometimes be invoked, as in the case of Samuel (cf. 1 Sam. 28: 8–25). But those who live in Sheol cannot thank Yahweh; only the living do so (cf. Is. 38: 18 f.; Ps. 88: 10–12). Consequently, ancestor-worship never figured in their religion. At the same time, we find references, in the Old Testament, to the king as the Son of God. God is said to have made a covenant with David through the prophet Nathan by which he would establish the kingdom of his "seed" after him. In that covenant God said: "I will be his father, and he shall be my son" (2 Sam. 7: 14). But Vriezen notes this was "probably owing to oriental court style" (as an adoption formula).[61] We have to wait for the appearance of Jesus Christ on earth to see the true instance of sonship to God.

The concepts we have been discussing, like several others which are present in African indigenous religions, are fundamentally foreign to those we find in the Old Testament about God and His relations to the world. We would therefore go on and say that the assumption that the Old Testament is on all fours with the African myths is far from accurate. For our present purposes, it seems clear that it was no accident that Jesus was born a Jew. The Jews, with about 2,000 years of the worship of Yahweh behind them, were a people who had been disciplined by the Law for about half that time. So "when the fulness of the times was come, God sent His Son, born of a woman, born under the Law to redeem those who were under the Law" (Gal. 4: 4). Significantly enough, He became the end of the Law (cf. Rom. 10: 4). St. Paul understood this fact in a unique way. In his epistles, the Jew in him, in keeping with the tradition of the Early Church, used Old Testament passages to establish the Messiahship of Jesus Christ. At the same time, the inferences he made from those passages were quite often at variance with their original contexts. His prime interest was to preach Jesus Christ and so he introduced conclusions germane to the Christian faith but which were built on a shift of interpretation of the passages quoted.[62] This point may be briefly illustrated from Romans and 1 Corinthians:

(i) *Romans* 1: 21

> "Although they knew God, they did not honour him as God
> or give thanks to him but they became futile in their thinking
> and their senseless minds were darkened." (R.S.V.)

The nearest Old Testament passage is that of Jeremiah 2: 5
which in LXX reads:

> "Thus says the Lord 'What fault did your fathers find in me
> that they stood afar from me and went after futilities and
> became futile?'"

The Jeremiah passage is obviously a rebuke directed against the
house of Jacob and all the families of the house of Israel because
of the deterioration of Israel's allegiance to Yahweh. "Israel was
once holiness to the Lord, the first fruits of his increase" (2: 3).
But now they have gone away "far from" Him (v. 5).

In Romans, the implications are directed against Gentiles.

(ii) *Romans* 2: 24

> "You who glory in the law through your transgression of the
> law do dishonour God [following Gifford]. For the name of
> God is blasphemed among the nations."

The parallel LXX passage is Isaiah 52: 5.

> "Thus said the Lord, because of you my name is blasphemed
> everywhere."

The Isaiah passage seems to refer to the disrepute to which God's
name is held by the Gentiles, who have taken the Israelites into
exile and oppressed them; obviously they are punished for their
sins. This leads to the inference (among the Gentiles) that their
gods seem to be superior to Yahweh (cf. Is. 36: 19). Some day,
however, God will arise and take a toll of the Gentiles to restore
His glory. "Therefore my people shall know my name; therefore
in that day they shall know that it is I who speak; here am I"
(Is. 52: 6 (R.S.V.), cf. Ez. 39: 7). In Romans the reference is to the
direct result of the violation of the Law by the Jews. God's name
is in disrepute, therefore, because the Jews show disregard of His

Law and of His Sovereignty and do so whilst living among Gentile peoples.

(iii) *Romans* 4: 6; *Ps.* 31: 1 (LXX)

"So also David pronounces a blessing upon the man to whom God reckons righteousness apart from works:
Blessed are those whose iniquities
are forgiven, and whose sins are covered
Blessed is the man against whom
the Lord will not reckon sin."

The LXX text of Psalm 31: 1 reads:

"Blessed are those whose iniquities (lawlessness) are forgiven and whose sins are covered. Blessed is the man of whom the Lord will not reckon sin and in whose mouth there is no guile."

The Romans passage is prefaced by an application of the doctrine of salvation, through faith apart from works of the Law, to the Old Testament passage. The original context of the Old Testament passage, on the other hand, points primarily to the blessings of forgiveness, blessings which come of the practice of the Law —St. Paul is obviously using the concept of justification to illuminate Psalm 31: 1. But the reference to David's pronouncing a blessing on "righteousness apart from works" is an intrusion into the context of the Psalm, of an interpretation foreign to the original background. The reference to God as "him who justifies the ungodly" (v. 5) is foreign to the Old Testament.[63]

(iv) *Romans* 4: 18

"So shall thy seed be."

This is an accurate quotation of the LXX of Gen. 15: 5.

In Genesis, the reference is to the future descendants of a child to be born to Abraham. In view of the Rabbinic emphasis on the birth of Isaac we would infer that the term "seed" was interpreted as referring to Isaac and not to Ishmael or the children of Keturah. This is the interpretation St. Paul gives to the term as seen in Gal. 3 : 16 f. At the same time, he introduces a new interpretation to the passage. Judging from Gal. 3 : 16 and Rom. 9 : 7, he first stressed the exclusive reference of the term, *seed*, to Isaac, and so, to Jesus Christ; He then fills out the picture by presenting Abraham in Rom. 4 as the Father of those Jews and Gentiles who believe in God who "raised from the dead Jesus our Lord, who was put to death for our trespasses and raised for our justification". In other words, St. Paul has introduced the diversity of Jews and Gentiles in the Unity of the Church—a concept unknown in the Old Testament. This interpretation can be applied to the complex of Abraham passages found in Romans 4 : 9, 11, 16 f., 18, 23 f. It may be added here that the term "faith" itself has two meanings. In the Old Testament, the term implies both an assentient as well as a fiduciary attitude. To believe in God is to accept that His word is true and to "rest in security and trustfulness upon Him". The Pauline usage is of a wider connotation. It embraces both the trust and confidence inherent in the Old Testament usage, especially so when used with reference to God, as well as the specifically Christian teaching that the Christian must have first died with Christ and have been buried into His death. Faith in this latter usage is a mystical relation between Christ and the Christian.

(v) *Romans* 5 : 4 f.

"Endurance produces character and character produces hope and hope does not disappoint us (make us ashamed) because God's love has been poured into our hearts through the Holy Spirit which has been given to us." (R.S.V.)

This passage is of special interest in this short study. There are four possible Old Testament passages which may have inspired this passage. Joel 2 : 27 f. (LXX)

". . . and my people will not be ashamed [καταισχυνθῶσαν] and it shall be afterwards that I will pour out [ἐκχεῶ] from my Spirit upon all flesh."

Or Psalm 22: 5 f. (21: 5 f.)

"In (Upon) thee our fathers hoped
They hoped and thou rescuedst them

.   .   .   .

In (Upon) thee they hoped and were not ashamed [κατησχυν
θήσαν]."

Or Psalm 25: 3, 20 (24: 3, 20)

"For all who endure thee will by no means be ashamed.
Let the lawless be ashamed because of their wantonness."
"Preserve thou my life [soul] and rescue me
Let me not be ashamed [καταισκυνθείην]
because I have hoped in thee."

Or Is. 28: 16 (LXX)

". . . Behold I lay for the foundations of Zion a cornerstone
precious and elect . . . and he who believes will by no means
be ashamed [καταισχυνθῇ]

א and A add "upon it" [ἐπ᾽ αὐτῷ] after "believes".

The last three passages are Messianic. Psalm 22: 5 describes
the confidence of the faithful believer in Yahweh; Isaiah 28: 16
stresses the steadfastness with which Yahweh establishes Zion,
and the Joel passage refers to the anticipation of the outpouring
of the Holy Spirit. The Romans passage, however, presents
endurance as character-forming, a character kept constant by the
cultivation of hope in Christ. This hope is eschatological, and is
anchored in Jesus Christ. (See Rom. 8: 24, 2 Cor. 3: 18, 4: 17;
1 Cor. 15: 19). St. Paul does know, of course, the Joel and
Isaiah passages because he uses them directly: Isaiah 28: 16 in
Romans 9: 33 and 10: 12, 13, Joel 2: 32 in Romans 10: 12, 13.
Romans 9: 32 follows the discussion which presents the Gentiles
as "adopting" faith. Although they had had no "law" to reveal
Yahweh's will to them, yet they had appropriated the blessings
of the righteous acts of God through the death and resurrection
of Jesus Christ. The Jews, on the other hand, enmeshed in their
legal obligations, had concerned themselves so much with

"works"—their own performance of righteous acts—that they had failed to discover the righteousness of God in Jesus Christ. St. Paul calls their mode of life a "blind" righteousness (cf. 10: 3) which they pursued as if the true righteousness of God, now demonstrated by Jesus Christ, could be attained by works (ὡς ἐξ ἔργων). Here, he is referring to righteousness in terms of a new yardstick and blames the Jews for their lack of sensibility to the new situation inaugurated by Jesus Christ. This insensibility has therefore caused them to fall "against the stone of stumbling". So he writes:

> "Behold I am laying in Zion a stone that will make men stumble
> a rock that will make them fall; and he who believes in him will not be put to shame" (Rom. 9: 33, R.S.V.)

St. Paul illustrates his point by blending the reference to the "stone of stumbling" found in Isaiah 8: 14 to the last sentence of the LXX of Isaiah 28: 16. In the LXX text of Isaiah 8: 14, the prophet "denies" the "stone of stumbling". The passage reads, "If you have confidence in him [i.e., the Lord God] he will be to you for a sanctuary and you will not encounter stumbling as of a stone nor a fall of a rock". St. Paul is obviously affirming it (the stone of stumbling), following the Massoretic text. A new application has thus been given to the passages. Professor James Denney notes that "the stone laid in Zion" in Isaiah 28: 16 refers to the "kingdom of promise as identified with its Sovereign Head" but "the stone of stumbling" in Isaiah 8: 14 "is unequivocally God Himself: all who do not give Him honour are broken against His government as on a stone or caught in it as a snare".[64] St. Paul however adds ἐπ' αὐτῷ after ὁ πιστεύων in both Romans passages, unless he had known the א and A versions of the LXX. In either case, by applying the language of Isaiah 28: 16, to Jesus Christ, he injects into the Old Testament texts a transference of ideas from Yahweh to Jesus Christ as the object of faith for the Christian.

Two further points must be noted: first, Isaiah 8: 14 is part of a message of assurance to the faithful witness of Yahweh, in the face of the humiliating situation caused by the submission of Ahaz to Tiglath-Pileser[65] and the resulting panic within the kingdom of Israel. Isaiah 28: 16 is part of a note of warning to "the drunkards of Ephraim" (28: 1) who claim immunity from death, whilst relying on a life of falsehood. Against this false confidence Yahweh pitted a true basis of confidence—a corner-stone, properly laid with line and plummet, viz.: justice and righteousness, which would expose the inevitable consequence of falsehood and injustice. The Romans passages, on the other hand, contrast the effect of faith and non-faith in Jesus Christ whose death on the cross has become a scandal to most of the Jews (cf. 1 Cor. 1: 23 f., 4: 9 f.). Thus St. Paul transcends the original implications of the passages—"assurance" from God and a life based on true "confidence" in God—by adapting them to depict the spiritual malaise which made the Jews reject Jesus Christ. "Blind" righteousness will naturally make those who live on that pattern stumble. The life of faith is, in fact, built on "grace" and is unattainable by any attempt to earn it by one's works.

Second, the Joel passage quoted in Romans 10: 12 f. begins with "and it shall be". St. Paul omits this and adds $\gamma\acute{\alpha}\varrho$ (for), thus implying that the Messianic hope of the prophecy has become an historical fact. So he transforms the reference to Yahweh to one relating to Jesus Christ. Leenhardt seems to us to short-circuit the argument when he suggests that this change implies the fact that "in the economy of salvation Paul does not distinguish between the work of Christ and that of God".[66] C. H. Dodd however claims that the conflation of Is. 28: 16 and 8: 14 already existed in a *Book of Testimonies* which Paul and the author of 1 Peter used. To him, both authors seem to have known the א and A versions of the LXX which affirm the "stone of stumbling" and the "rock of tripping".[67] This may be so. But as Barrett points out, "Paul was not unfamiliar with the Old Testament, and it must be supposed that he knew what he was doing when he used the composite quotation, which contains in germ the argument developed in X: 1–13".[68]

(vi) *Romans* 14: 11

". . . it is written,
As I live says the Lord, every knee shall bow to me,
and every tongue shall give praise to God." (R.S.V.)

This quotation is from Is. 45: 23 (LXX):

"By myself do I swear; only righteousness shall proceed
out of my mouth. My words will not depart from me viz.;
that every knee shall bow to me and every tongue shall swear
[by] God saying, righteousness and glory will come to him and
all who disturb [are incensed against] them shall be ashamed."

St. Paul has made material changes in the LXX text of Is. 45: 23.
He substitutes "As I live saith the Lord" probably from Is.
49: 18 for the LXX "By myself do I swear"; he omits the following two sentences and goes direct to the noun clause, but he also
alters "every tongue shall swear by God" (ἐξομολογήσεται),
to "every tongue shall give praise" to God (ὀμεῖται . . . . τὸν
θεὸν). We may here draw attention to Stauffer's observation
that God's call to the nations—an invitation leading on to a
threat—has been turned by St. Paul into "a summons, the grave
summons to the last judgment".[69] It is significant that this
Isaiah passage is used in Phil. 2: 10 with a different modification
in a Christological setting in which the Apostle describes the
universal lordship of Christ over all creation,

"that at the name of Jesus every knee should bow, in heaven
and on earth and under the earth." (R.S.V.)

Here the Apostle makes "all bend the knee, angels in heaven,
men on earth and shades of the underworld", all "join without
exception in the chorus of those who confess Christ".[70]

(vii) 1 *Cor.* 11: 8 f.

"Man was not made from woman, but woman from man.
Neither was man created for woman but woman for man."
(R.S.V.)

This passage is obviously based on Gen. 2: 21–23:

"The Lord God caused a deep sleep to fall upon the man, and while he slept took one of his ribs and closed up its place with flesh; and the rib which the Lord God had taken from the man he made into a woman and brought her to the man. . . ." (R.S.V.)

St. Paul however injects a Christian interpretation into the Genesis story of Creation by adding in 11:11,

"Nevertheless in the Lord woman is not independent of man nor man of woman; for as woman was made from man, so man is now born of woman" (R.S.V.)

perhaps a reference to the virgin birth of Jesus Christ. St. Paul is obviously going beyond the point of reference of the Genesis story and in effect reversing the whole process.

(viii) 1 *Cor.* 11:7

"For a man ought not to cover his head, since he is the image and glory of God; but woman is the glory of man." (R.S.V.)

The argument supporting woman wearing the veil is based on Gen. 2:21–23. But after following it up to a point, St. Paul reverts to a different basis—that of nature.

"Does not nature itself teach you", he continues, "that for a man to wear long hair is degrading to him, but if a woman has long hair, it is her pride? For her hair is given to her for a covering." (v. 14) (R.S.V.)

The religious argument now gives way to an argument from nature, obviously because St. Paul could not sustain it and still maintain the language of Gal. 3:28.

"There is neither Jew nor Greek, there is neither slave nor free, there is neither male nor female; for you are all one in Christ Jesus." (R.S.V.)

The question therefore arises, How far is Roland Allen correct in stating that St. Paul took around the Old Testament which he delivered to his converts?[71] Was it not more likely that St.

Paul, brought up in the Jewish religion and nurtured in the Jewish scriptures, first drew upon the rich mine of piety and religious instruction of his religious world and later strove to adapt his knowledge and religious devotional life to the Christian idiom? If, as we would suggest, this interpretation is more acceptable, then we have in the Pauline Epistles a *modus operandi* for preaching the Christian Gospel to Africans who do not possess the basic attitudes to God which we know the Jews possessed. In other words, the Jewish understanding of God as a God of History, who intervenes in the life and experiences of human beings and as the God who inspires His prophets to teach their people the true content of His Will, is the prime basis of a full understanding of that manifestation in Jesus Christ which took place at the Incarnation, as well as of a grasp of the love which prompted God to reconcile man to Himself.

For the writer, the inevitable inference must be that the Christian evangelist, as well as the members of the ordained ministry, must so understand the basic teachings of the Old Testament that they can appreciate the unique Jewish concept of God. This, to us, is the bridge between the religious ideas of the pagan world and Christianity. Too much time must not, however, be spent at this stage on questions of suitable curricula. It is doubtful whether the Greek converts of St. Paul necessarily understood the Old Testament language he used, in terms of the contexts of the passages cited. It does seem possible that intelligent Greeks could understand most of the passages without first having been proselytes with some knowledge of the Septuagint. We would add that this interpretation of the situation of the Gentile churches should lead to a reconsideration of the study of the Old Testament in theological colleges. Future clergy and ministers should in our opinion be helped to acquire a real grasp of the tenets of the Jewish religion so that they may satisfactorily understand the changes implicit in the New Testament usages.[72] Whilst Professor Godfrey Phillips may be correct in stating that the great words of the New Testament, e.g., Atonement, Reconciliation, Forgiveness, all come from the Old Testament, we would also urge that their uses in the New Testament far outstrip those in the Old Testament scriptures. For the African Christian evangelist, the New Testament must be his guide.

Postscript

One further point which calls for greater discussion than is possible in this work is that there seem to be two concepts of God held in some tension. First, the idea that God was part of the world but later left it—as seen in the myths extant among the Mende of Sierra Leone, the Akan of Ghana, the Yoruba of Nigeria and the Bapedi. Here, God is identical with the world and directs the fate and destinies of men. So both good and evil forces are traceable to Him. The day and night sky manifest His power. This notion does not, strictly speaking, emphasize God's immanence. It primarily emphasizes His identity with the world. God is in this context the essence of cosmic totality. He is thus man's Great Ancestor. Divine kingship seems to have originated from this notion. Second, God is represented as Creator, thus describing Him as separate and distinct from the world. He is therefore a Judge who makes moral demands of man. One is left wondering whether this explains why God is called by more than one name, e.g., the Akan, *Nyame*, *Nyankopon*, *Odomankoma*; or the Mende, *Ŋgewɔ* and *Leve*; or the Yoruba, *Olodumare* and *Ɔlɔrun*.[73] The Creator-concept seems to be later than the ancestor-concept, but far more work must first be done before a clearer picture can be attained.

E

Chapter 3

SOUND DOCTRINAL TEACHING—I

"THE CHRISTIAN GOSPEL offers life-saving news about the whole range of personal and social life; about God, man and society, in the only way in which it could be really clear to men. It has been once for all embodied in a Life, in and through which God has offered, and still offers, the light, power, deliverance, and fellowship to meet men's deepest needs. For all who will accept it, and order their lives by it, it is the one way to abundant victorious life."[1]

So Christians maintain that in Jesus Christ are combined the revelation of God to man, His love, His power and His suffering, as well as the redemption of man by God, leading to man's forgiveness and adoption to sonship. In Jesus Christ we also have the perfect exemplar of man's total obedience to the will of God, His will being in full *rapport* with the will of God.

This revelation of God once-for-all in Jesus Christ is, however, being continued today in varying proportions by the influence of the Holy Spirit who leads redeemed humanity into a life of sanctification (1 Thess. 4: 3 ff.; Romans 8: 11 f., 14–30, Gal. 4: 6 f., 5: 16–26). He it is who increases the Christian's understanding of God, of his salvation in Jesus and His present will for the Church.[2] Our Lord's mission, as is well known, demanded of Him the total consecration of all His powers towards the complete obedience to the will of God[3] (John 17: 19; Romans 15: 3). This obedience must naturally be reflected in the life of the Church (John 17: 19) as His Body. In view of the inherent sinfulness of human nature, such obedience requires a transformation from a life of total rebelliousness, to one of obedience; that is, a "transformation of the unholy into the holy". Hence

St. Paul enjoined his Roman readers to "be transformed by the renewal of the mind" (cf. Romans 12: 2). This transformation can only take place in the Church,[4] and results in "a new creation", which embraces not only the moral agents of the world, but also the whole of God's creation.[5]

In this work, then, the term "transfiguration" implies the total surrender of man's thoughts and habits, his creativity and his worship, in the march towards taking captive every thought and making it obedient to Christ (2 Cor. 10: 5). In our view, this surrender depends upon two constituent factors which deserve a high place in any programme of building up a healthy Church life in Africa:

(a) Sound doctrine, i.e., the teaching by which Christians are led to possess and so to impart to others that body of knowledge which teaches man that God is a God who is motivated by love to speak and act, and

(b) Worship, i.e., man's humble and grateful response in a manner appropriate to the voice of God.[6]

In the present chapter, we shall describe certain features of the nature of such a sound doctrine as we have in mind.

(i) An Intelligent Study of the Scriptures

We would affirm that if Christianity is to be identified with the culture of African peoples it is imperative that the Church in Africa keeps its place in the family of the universal Church; it must therefore ensure that the scriptures continue to be her norm in order to preserve her contact with the apostolic tradition of the Church as well as with the rich contribution of various generations of Christians who have hitherto ministered to every age and culture. She must accordingly learn always to study and interpret the scriptures in a way adequate to set forth the truth as it is in Jesus, according to her special needs. This is her surest guarantee that she will continue to be "rooted and grounded" in the faith of the Church universal and at the same time be competent to satisfy her contemporary needs at any one time.

Again, Christianity is a religion which demands the full use of the intellect of its adherents. The Christian must not only learn of the ministry of Jesus, he must understand His teachings. To this end, he must be helped first to enter upon a true study of the Scriptures and thereby attain a clear understanding of the Person of Jesus Christ.

Otherwise the church in Africa would isolate herself from the rest of the Church. We would say with William Nicholls that "to ignore the breadth of the tradition of the Church means becoming the prisoner of one's own culture".[7] Nicholls also asserts that "authentic tradition, beginning with the rule of faith, going on to the creeds, and including the theological developments of every cultural embodiment of the faith, is the proper and indispensable key to the understanding of Scripture".[8] Unless African Christians remain in the main stream of the tradition of the Church they cannot claim to belong to the world-wide Church. Hence the wisdom of the comment that "whatever the difficulties in the presentation of Church History to Africans, its importance as a subject cannot . . . be too highly rated. At a time when the tendency to create new 'sects' and 'splinter groups' is all too obvious, the need for an understanding of Church History is all the greater."[9]

On the strength of this argument we can see, for example, the importance of helping African clergy and ministers to grasp the significance of the term *homoousion* in the Nicene Creed. Otherwise, they would by-pass a historical element of the highest importance in the Christian Tradition. The writer's own teaching experience has taught him that a study of the early heresies of the Church is of much relevance today, when silhouetted against the growing agnosticism and naïve approach of young African scientists to religious questions. Some of the current themes which are in danger of being overlooked in any other system are: "Is God the Creator of the Universe?" "Does God suffer? If so, how?" "Could Jesus have been born of Mary without the intervention of a human father?" "Was Jesus truly human and yet truly divine?" To many of the increasing body of young scientists in Africa the notions of cause and effect, now interpreted in terms of the physical sciences, tend to create a cynicism which unfortunately undermines their native beliefs and at the same time makes the acceptance of Christianity ludicrous. Unless there is a body of Christian thinking founded upon the tradition of the Church, Christianity will find no buttress against which the thrust of secularist thinking can become ineffective.

Considerations like those mentioned above lead us to call attention to the dangers of fundamentalist biblical teaching in Africa. William Nicholls points out that "the fundamentalist churches ... suppose that they can by-pass tradition and go direct to Scripture, but also in fact all unknowingly become terribly provincial and narrow in their interpretation of it, and in consequence very unfitted for the missionary role for which they cast themselves".[10] Fundamentalism is of course difficult to define, because it is used differently by different people, as for example in Great Britain, vis-à-vis the United States of America.[11] Judging from *The Times* correspondence of 1955, Biblical fundamentalists do have a powerful evangelistic influence; at the same time they are exclusive and intolerant and are therefore accused of not giving enough attention to the place of "reason and revelation" in the religious experience. This attitude is fraught with serious difficulties for the modern intellectual, some of which we may mention here.

(ii) PROBLEMS OF BIBLICAL FUNDAMENTALISM

First, Biblical fundamentalism ignores the revelation which has come to the world through the researches of scientists and takes refuge in the assumption that "the Bible is infallibly authoritative". It accepts the story of the Creation in the first three chapters of Genesis as literally true and ignores the discoveries of geologists and astronomers.[12] This attitude can scarcely convince the growing intellectuals of Africa. For the Church to cultivate the respect of the young African scientists, she must "always be ready for reason to throw fresh, and perhaps modifying, light upon what we have hitherto regarded as revelation".[13] Indeed, as has been well said, "Authority is enhanced by revelation". Second, as was pointed out in *The Times* correspondence of 1955, some fundamentalists tend to lay emphasis on "a comfortable certitude of heavenly bliss here-after", whilst they offer little or no guidance on the meaning in this life, here and now, of the Gospel Sayings of Jesus.[14] They thus tend to stress the emotional whilst they neglect the rational factors of the religious life. Third, extreme Biblical fundamental-ism is generally anti-Church. That is to say that it leads men away from the fellowship which the Church engenders to individualism. Such an attitude is, of course, disastrous for the growth of Church life in Africa.[15]

It is significant that one pro-fundamentalist writer in *The Times* correspondence expressed the view that "the non-Christian millions of Asia, Africa and Europe will never be reached" by those who are "trying to teach Christianity as a kind of subject like higher mathematics". So, he goes on, "They want some-thing simple, effective, dynamic, and alive—the Gospel message of the Bible clearly and authoritatively presented with the power of God behind it".[16] We would say with the next writer, "it (Fundamentalism) meets an obvious psychological need, but by a very dangerous prescription which may cure the symptom only to kill the patient".[17] The Church in Africa must never be guilty of the comment once made on the Church in England that "so many evangelistic campaigns designed to reach 'the people' give the man-in-the-street little or no credit for ability to think for himself on religious matters".[18] We would therefore urge that, if the Encounter of the Church is to be real and complete, African Christians must be helped to surrender their reason and their emotions equally to Christ (cf. 2 Cor. 10: 5; Mark 12: 29 f.).

Second, chiefly because of fundamentalist attitudes, Christian preaching in Africa today (1968) tends to be so much moralizing that the primitive Kerygma naturally becomes a secondary evangelistic instrument. To be effective, Christian preaching and teaching should demonstrate the fact that moral demands are inevitable corollaries of the essential Christian tenets. In par-ticular, the African Christian should be helped to realize that Jesus Christ is the end and goal of all revelation, and, therefore,

He must not be worshipped as one of several deities. Pluralism has no place in Christianity. Where, as in Africa, morality is associated with the lesser deities, there is a quest for a new deity, preferably of some reputation, in a neighbouring territory, to whom resort may be made, when the local deities fail to be effective. A never-ending search thus goes on. So Mrs. Meyerowitz, writing of the Akan in 1951, observed, "Today, with the increased incidence of sterility arising from the spread of venereal disease, people, disappointed with their gods and with Christianity, are turning to foreign 'fetish' gods, introduced from the north, which promise by their magical powers to be more effective than *ntorɔ*", because of their desire to have a child.[19] Dr. Kofi Busia calls attention to a like situation in his study of the *Tigare* cult in Sekondi (Ghana).[20] The *Tigare* cult came to Sekondi from the French Ivory Coast via the Northern Territories of Ghana.

Margaret Field paints an amusing picture when she says of the Ga, "Among the great invisible gods who hold Ga property in their hands has come a *new* (italics, mine), great, invisible god of less calculable and less tolerant quality, namely 'Gov'ment'. From his fabulously wealthy, heavenly home across the water he sends his gifts and his emissaries". She then goes on to describe some of the activities of this *new* god, viz.: the provision of Chinese rice in times of famine, pipe-borne water, road-making. "These are not fruits of the earth as normal food is, but arrive mysteriously from nowhere". "Gov'ment" now proves superior to *La Kpa*, the head god of Labadi, as it can counter any penalties like famine and drought.[21] Obviously these and other similar cases call for a Christian approach in depth which would expose the futility of the belief in the so-called deities, whilst inculcating in African Christians the special significance of the Revelation in Jesus Christ as the Agent of Creation and the king-pin on which everything in the world hangs together. In other words, careful instruction on the significance of the Incarnation becomes a *desideratum*.

(iii) The Uniqueness of the Incarnation of Jesus Christ for Christian Evangelism in Africa

In the African situation the Incarnation should be so presented as to emphasize that Jesus Christ was the manifestation of God's love for man, God's share in human sufferings, God's victory over death and all the disastrous influences which throng man's everyday experiences. In short, African Christians should be helped to realize that Jesus Christ was born as *I* was, grew up as *I* did, perhaps with all the innocent mischief found in a growing boy or girl, and was later persecuted by His contemporaries because He was fully dedicated to the service of God; He therefore suffered death because of His unflinching loyalty to God. But God raised Him from the dead because He was "that Man in whom God lived, and acted (and still does act) humanwise".[22] In this way, we could affirm our Lord's affinity to man as a basis for presenting the Church as "the Great Family", of which Jesus Christ is the Head.

Christian Africans will thus be able to find in the Church that unifying influence which transcends tribe and clan, and particularly the many divisive influences which national independence tends to engender. The Church as the Body of Christ represents the *primum ens* from which all Christians take their origin, and so tribal affiliations of Christians give way to the totality of the community of the Church, with Jesus Christ as its first member.

This interpretation of the role of Jesus Christ as that of an elder brother seems to be more readily acceptable, and certainly more salutary, than Paul de Fueter's suggestion that Jesus Christ should be presented to African converts and enquirers as chief. Fueter says: "We preach Christ who is the real chief, the king for Africa. He is the ruler who comes and in whose presence all is forgotten, with whom one is secure for ever."[23] We would suggest that Chiefship is particularly vulnerable as a description of Jesus Christ because: (*a*) Chiefs lost their pristine power and influence in the old days of colonial rule; in the new independent states, their positions are, generally speaking, quite precarious. (*b*) Chiefship does not, *per se*, imply unquestioned supreme rule.

It has never done. The chief is always answerable to his council of Elders who in a measure determine his tenure of office. Absolute despotism was never tolerated. The despot either lost his life or was compelled to commit suicide; at best he was deposed.[24] (c) The chiefs of African tribesmen have never been readily accessible to the ordinary man. Under normal circumstances, chiefs must be approached through middlemen with official titles, e.g., Ɔkyeame, among the Akan, *Bangura*, among the Temne of Sierra Leone, *Balogun*, among the Yoruba, *Lavale* (mouthpiece), among the Mende of Sierra Leone. Even gifts offered to the chief have to be presented through middlemen. At court, as among the Mende, they are the official spokesmen. Only when a suppliant approaches the chief, *not* in his judicial capacity, but as *father-protector*, is there direct access to him. (d) Again, chiefs generally live in a walled settlement and are therefore not exposed to the ordinary contacts of their subjects. Thus, for example, in former times, the *Alafin* of Oyo went out on official circuits veiled, and the king of Dahomey was never seen whilst having his meals. The Akan king made very few public appearances so that the evil wishes of his subjects might not injure his *kra* and so expose him to death.

We therefore suggest that chiefship is unsuited to the Person of Christ. But to represent Jesus Christ as the first-born among many brethren who with Him together form the Church is in true keeping with African notions. For Christians, an effort must be made to bring home the mystical relation between Christ and the Christian which St. Paul talks of in Gal. 2: 19 ff.

This mystical relation with Christ has many important implications which deserve a separate treatment. We may, however, isolate a few:

(i) SONSHIP WITH GOD

By it we are adopted into sonship with God, because, as St. Paul tells us, Jesus Christ was ordained by God to become the first-born among many brethren. Christians are equally ordained to be conformed (shaped, N.E.B.) to the likeness of Jesus Christ (cf. Romans 8: 29, 1 John 3: 2). This is man's true destiny.

This new relationship will, in our view, provide the means of overcoming the deeply ingrained feeling of insecurity which creates acute social and psychological problems among even Christian Africans. The non-Christian African feels insecure and frustrated, but he has a ready-made formula for dealing with his difficulties, be they sudden or inexplicable deaths, especially so of children, or sterility or bad success. He presumes witchcraft, or a spirit, cultic, ancestral or demonic, and performs the appropriate religious rites which restore his self-confidence, and all is well again.[25] The various spirits are, however, attempts to establish concrete manifestations of deity. To the Christian, this attitude is obviously *idolatrous*. The pagan, however, understands his situation and can deal appropriately, sometimes adequately, with the spirits and deities involved. For him there is a visible manifestation of the presence of the spirits near to hand in the form of a totem, an idol, or the memory of the ancestors; he understands the rule of life they require, and the compensations they impose in cases of violation of that rule. He also knows that they have no pity, but can be propitiated. More so, he knows how to dodge them. When, however, he becomes a Christian and is faced with a situation which breeds insecurity, he can no longer fall back on the old familiar ways of solving his problem, because he does not find available any concrete manifestations whose aid he can press into service. He may be willing to give up his pagan beliefs and so cultivate a genuine confidence in God. But an attitude of total surrender to God seems difficult to sustain after two generations. The answer to this problem is to be found, in our view, in the Christian doctrine of the Incarnation.

(ii) Jesus Christ the Agent of Creation

(a) Although the spirits worshipped in Africa may be said to be close to and, therefore, the agents of God, yet they are not God. They may, as in the case of *Orunmila*, reveal the will of God to man, but they are not human. At best, they can only be described as intermediaries, serving like electrical sub-stations, between God and man. Another deity, *Orisa-nla*, is said to have fashioned man, but he did not give life to the forms. On the other hand, Christianity asserts that God created the world with Jesus Christ as the agent both of the first creation and of the New Creation. In the Christian era, therefore, we are helped to discover first that in Jesus Christ "the complete being of the Godhead dwells embodied. ... Every power and authority in the universe is subject to him as Head" (Col. 2: 10, N.E.B.). "The whole universe has been created through and for him" (Col. 1: 16, N.E.B.). In Him the Logos of God "became flesh" ... and men "saw his glory" (cf. John 1: 14; 1 John 1: 1 f.). At the same time, because we are Christians, we have been "brought into completion" in Him. Indeed, the Christian doctrine of the Incarnation presents Jesus Christ to us as a genuine ladder between God and nature, man included, His head fully contained within the Godhead and His feet firmly planted on earth by His perfect humanity. So in Jesus Christ we have the concrete manifestation of Godhead. In the language of Professor Leonard Hodgson, "In Jesus Christ, we see God at work in the history of this world, personally incarnate for the purpose of rescuing His creation from the evil with which it had become infected".[26] Because He was human, He was by nature superior to man-made idols. They have no life and no direction of purpose. Indeed, they lead men to futile thinking and so to dither, hither and thither. On the other hand, in Jesus Christ was life and He was a life-giving spirit. Even His words are "spirit and life" (cf. Romans 1: 21, 1 Cor. 12: 2, John 6: 63; cf. Jer. 5). This aspect of the Incarnation, as the supreme instance of the concrete manifestation of deity, naturally supersedes all other hierophanies and affords the Christian the means of realizing his true destiny. In Jesus Christ, God "chose us before the world was founded. ..." This belief leads to moral demands. "We are God's handiwork, created in Christ Jesus to devote ourselves to the good deeds for which God has designed us" (Eph. 2: 10, N.E.B.).

(b) We recall that belief in spirits leads to certain moral requirements of the devotees. But this tendency is even more true of the Christian religion with its emphasis on God as *holy* and morally reliable. For the Christian, these characteristics are manifested in Jesus Christ who is the *Yes* of God (2 Cor. 1: 18 ff.). So the Christian, like the pagan, is enjoined not to "lie to one another", to adjure "fornication, indecency, lust, foul cravings and ruthless greed" (cf. Col. 3: 5, N.E.B.). Unlike the pagan, however, his behaviour is determined by his relation to Jesus Christ through baptism. So the basis of the new life he should lead is his baptism into Christ's death and the subsequent resurrection to newness of life (Romans 6: 3 f., Col. 2: 12). He is, therefore, told to "put to death" the evil life he had lived in the past and "put on the new nature which is being constantly renewed in the image of its Creator and brought to know God" (Col. 3: 5 –10, N.E.B.); on this basis, sin acquires a new criterion. It is not determined by mere motive and intention, but on a deeper basis of one's personal relationship with Jesus Christ (1 John 5: 1; Rom. 6: 11).

(c) Equally, repentance is no longer merely a question of confession and regret of past actions; it is a re-creation of man's nature according to the pattern of Christ, leading to a total surrender of the self to God. This surrender involves an experience of God through experience of Jesus Christ, referred to in Col. 3: 10 as knowledge of God. As a result of this re-creation, the bodies of Christians are the "limbs and organs of Christ", so they can no longer be used for lustful ends. Ruthless greed by which an individual unscrupulously sacrifices the interests of others for his own good is loathsome among pagans. But, for Christians, it assumes a grosser nature. Indeed, it constitutes idolatry (cf. Col. 3: 5; Eph. 5: 5; 1 Cor. 5: 10, 6: 10 f.) because it indicates the futile thinking which comes of trying to put oneself in place of God. Again, anxiety bred by fear, as we have already noted, is, most of the time, the driving force which leads pagan Africans to the worship of the spirits and deities. It is, therefore, not enough to say to the African convert that faith in Jesus Christ dispels fear—quoting, perhaps in support of this, our Lord's victory over the demons. No doubt a confirmed faith in Jesus Christ does dispel anxiety. But the doctrine of the Incarnation provides other answers which fill out the references to our Lord's victory over demons. These answers can be found in our Lord's own personal attitude to God. St. Luke tells us that our Lord usually spent a night in prayer alone, before undertaking any major action, and the story of Gethsemane is the perfect example of our Lord's behaviour at a time of imminent crisis. He went and prayed alone, three times. Here is one clue to the Christian's attitude to crises. But crises are not always averted by prayer; they often come to pass, as in the case of our Lord's arrest.

(d) Our understanding of this point provides one major difference between the Christian's attitude to prayer and that which dominates prayers to the spirits. Pagan prayers are uttered on the assumption that a positive and often immediate answer will be received if the appropriate ritual is performed and the correct words uttered. This is particularly true of the piacular rites. We would say that the Incarnation of Jesus Christ helps us to see the true attitude to suffering; Jesus Christ, the God-man, "learned obedience through the school of suffering"; "he offered up prayers and petitions, with loud cries and tears" (Heb. 5: 7 f., N.E.B.). He was tested every way, "only without sin" (N.E.B.), because He was like one of us. He died and was buried like any one of us. But God raised Him from the dead. Through Him, therefore, Deity had assumed manhood and so understood the meaning of human suffering, even to the point of dying like we do. The Incarnation thus leads us to the inference that God can and does stand in with us in the hour of our greatest suffering; at the same time it holds out to us the promise of a new life if we are prepared to share in our Lord's sufferings (cf. Rom. 8: 17), a relationship which begins at our baptism. Thus we can in times of anxiety take a leaf from Jesus Christ's behaviour. Anxiety turns the pagan to improvise his own solution of his problems, sometimes invoking the aid of God. The Christian, on the other hand, turns his attention towards God in total surrender to the Will of God. His faith in Jesus Christ assures him of victory.

Where the right kind of instruction on the problem of suffering is given to the African convert, he is helped to see two things: first, that he need not begin to scout around through diviners to discover what spirits or deities he has offended, and, second, that in his sufferings God Himself understands his situation. Indeed, he can count on the moral support of Jesus Christ whatever his difficulties may be. We are therefore in a position to counter the belief in witchcraft, particularly so, that form which, as Dr. Margaret Field and Debrunner suggest, is primarily based on anxiety and depression.[27]

(e) Again, African society in contemporary times seems to lack a balanced and settled attitude to life. Indeed, there seems to be a fall from the standards of conduct implicit in tribal life. For Father Tempels, the answer to this problem is one of adaptation—adaptation to the ontology of the African; the Bantu in this context. He contends further that the "évolué and often the Christian has never effected a reconciliation between his new way of life and his former philosophy".[28] Hence, there are, according to Fr. Tempels, so many déracinés in the Congo, for example, many materialists and a large majority who remain "under the light coating of white imitation".[29] He therefore suggests that "missionaries, magistrates, administrators, all in directive posts or posts which ought to be directive have failed to reach" the souls of the Africans, thus failing to produce for them "a purer and a more dynamic life".[30] This situation, to the author, explains the religious pluralism of baptized Bantus.[31]

Similarly, H. Debrunner writing about Ghana contends, "Unless superseded by a deep Christian conviction and a true conversion, traditional religion is not easily discarded" by the African convert. So the young Ghanaian who goes to school first of all becomes the object of jealousy and spite "among his compatriots and therefore feels he is being bewitched". He continues, "In view of the all too rapid spread of education mostly sponsored by the Churches, traditional religion is very often formally abandoned by the young literates who are without a deep inner conviction".[32] So, not finding education a "magic key" to success, they see enemies everywhere. Quoting an eminent Ghanaian music teacher, he says, "The simple truth is that superstition and the fear of evil spirits is as strong as ever today among Christians, literates and illiterates alike. What is still more distressing is that the fear of the evil consequences of immorality which once existed with superstition, and the fear of evil spirits have been dispelled by Christianity and education."[33] Dr. Idowu of Nigeria voices a similar opinion. He regrets the disappearance of the "direct ritualistic worship of *Olodumare*" as a regular feature of Yoruba life; commenting later, on the impact of western influence on the Yoruba, he writes, "Western influence has not been altogether beneficial to the people. . . . Christianity, by a miscarriage of purpose, makes its own contribution to the detrimental changes in moral values. Somehow, it has replaced the old fear of the divinities with the relieving but harmful notion of a God who is a sentimental Old Man, ever ready to forgive perhaps even more than man is prone to sin, the God in whom 'Goodness and severity' have been put asunder".[34] Those who feel a concern for a real impact of Christianity on Africa must pay heed to Fr. Tempels and Debrunner, even if they are not prepared to go the whole way with Idowu.[35]

(iii) Jesus Christ the Founder of the Great Family— the Church

(a) St. Paul tells us that Christians *qua* Christians are all "one man" in Christ Jesus without distinction of race, sex, colour or condition (Gal. 3: 28; cf. Eph. 2: 11–22; John 17: 21); they have all been made to drink of (irrigated by) one spirit, the Holy Spirit, at baptism (1 Cor. 12: 13), and are intimate sharers of the one body and blood of Christ (1 Cor. 10: 16 f.).

In every case the Church is the body of Christ and Christ is the head of the Church (Eph. 1: 22; Col. 1: 18); the Church is a temple built upon the foundation of the apostles and prophets, Jesus Christ Himself being the chief corner-stone (Eph. 2: 20). All Christians together form God's royal household (1 Pet. 2: 9). And so, "if any man is in Christ, there is a new creation" (2 Cor. 5: 17, R.V. marg.). If, then, as Leonard Hodgson points out, this "new creation" factor of the Church is a manifestation of evolutionary features, by spreading out both to and in Africa, the Church is extending the sphere of influence of "Christ at work in the world. . . ."[36] Again, if the Church means the *Totus Christus, membra cum capite*, then its universality is axiomatic in the teaching of the New Testament. We would therefore go on to assert that the Church is "the whole congregation of Christian people dispersed throughout the whole world",[37] each local congregation "being the Universal Church of Christ in this place".[38]

In the language of 1 Corinthians 12: 12 f., the Church is an organism manifesting a unity in a diversity. That is to say, it consists of distinct individualities expressive of "a capacity for variation and mutation which is uniquely creative and original".[39] Such originality is based on the fact that

> "The Church is His [Christ's] Body, the fullness of Him who is in all respects being fulfilled" (Eph. 1: 23).[40]

Or in the language of Dr. Wand's translation:

> "That Body [the Church] provides a universal means of expression for one who is Himself a universal personality".[41]

This universality can be described in terms of the sensitivity of Christianity to its cultural environment, a sensitivity manifested (a) distributively, by the impact of the environment,[42] and (b) collectively by the total deposit of the cultural accretions which have contributed to Christianity through the ages—Jewish Christianity with which there has been an interaction of Syrian, Alexandrian, Roman, Gallic, Celtic, Anglo-Saxon and Indian and other cultures. In this context, the Christianization of Africa should mean not merely a transplantation of cultures from cultures foreign to Africa but the integration of African culture into the fabric of Christianity, thereby adding a new dimension to the already complex polyhedra. In this way, the Church in Africa will be encouraged to develop an originality of its own, provided it does not lead to a syncretism "compromising the (Christian) revelation with the surrounding culture, and", more so, "with the non-Christian religion which has bound it together".[43] Indeed, Christianity cannot be "identified with any of the types of culture in which it is successively embodied"[44] because it "requires, always, both an incarnation and a detachment".[45]

Many Europeans are conscious of the need of the originality which we have mentioned but one wonders how far they have given the question serious thought. A glaring instance of this is seen in the somewhat naïve insistence by some on depicting Christ as an African. For an African child, who has never understood the significance of the fact that Jesus was born a Jew, it would be natural to draw a picture of Christ as an African. Equally so, one would understand a poet who, fired by his love for Africa—through sympathy, in the case of a foreigner, or through patriotism, in the case of an African—expressed the wish that Jesus Christ had been born of a black Mary. Such a wish would be pardonable poetic licence.[46] But for adult Christians who understand Bible history and indeed the significance of what has been termed "the stumbling block of particularity", an African Christ is a travesty of the process by which God led mankind to salvation from the power of sin (Rom. 9: 4 f.). We recognize that members of the secessionist Churches have been known to have said, "Jesus came first as a white man. But now he has come as a black man, in the flesh. . . ."[47] This statement is, of course, theological nonsense.

(b) Again, Christianity in Africa has always stressed monogamy and denounced the customary practice of polygamy. But questions are being asked today by Europeans and Africans alike as to whether polygamy is inconsistent with Christianity. E. A. Asamoa of Ghana, for example, whilst admitting that "though polygamy is quite a legitimate form of marriage (in Africa), the large majority of men marry one wife",[48] also makes the strong comment that "it is a controversial question whether the New Testament has anything to say against polygamy as such, even by implication". For him, the fact that "the New Testament does not issue injunctions about particular patterns of life which Christians are called upon to adopt shows indeed the uniqueness and universality of the Christian religion, and is in

F

accordance with the spirit of Christianity, which is 'life' and not 'form'. . . . Mere form," he continued, "whether of monogamy or polygamy, can be 'dead'. Inspired by the spirit of Christ, the form, whether of monogamy or polygamy, can 'live'. The form need not change in order to live."[49]

In 1960 Mr. Lisle Ramsey, President of the Religious Heritage of America, on his return from an eight-week tour of Africa, is reported to have said that "the Christian Churches should work out some means so that a man can be accepted even if he has more than one wife. Unless Christianity has the vision to accept Christians in their present environment, then Christianity will lose Africa, and Africa will lose any chance of freedom."[50] Mr. Ramsey's real concern seemed to have been the prospect of the Church losing Africa to Islam. To the writer, both Asamoa and Lisle Ramsey's statements are most tendentious.

At the same time, the problem of childlessness among African couples calls for some attention. In communities where, as among the Jews, childlessness is regarded as a social privation, the childless woman in some cases encourages her husband to marry a second wife in the hope of his begetting a child by her (cf. Gen. 16: 1-4). Dr. G. Parrinder and Canon J. V. Taylor, both missionaries of long experience and knowledge of Africa, therefore look sympathetically on polygamy from this angle.[51] We would question the accuracy of the comment that there are no injunctions about monogamy in the New Testament; the careful reader will readily appreciate that the Pauline injunctions about marriage in 1 Corinthians are sometimes based on the authority of Jesus (1 Cor. 7: 10 ff.). In particular, the language of Ephesians 5: 23-33 could scarcely be more explicitly monogamous both in intent, and in the recurrent use of the singular 'wife' (cf. 1 Cor. 7; 1 Thess. 4: 1-6).

Certainly, if the relation of Christ to His Church could be accurately presented in material language, as in Ephesians 5: 32, we may rightly conclude that the Asamoas and Lisle Ramseys are fired by ideas which are contrary to the spirit of the New Testament and therefore of Christianity.[52] We sympathize with the Parrinders and J. V. Taylors; but we also think that the

Rt. Rev. A. W. Howells, late Bishop of Lagos, sounded the healthier note when he said, at the Anglican Congress in Minneapolis in 1954, that "West Africa has not yet faced the challenge of monogamy, the Christian ideal of marriage and the relationship of man to woman".[53] Already, the spread of secondary and higher education among women is creating such social changes as to threaten the continuance of polygamy even among the Moslems, certainly in the urban areas. Unlike their illiterate sisters, educated wives assume, without qualification, that their husbands should maintain them. Monogamy is, accordingly, steadily gaining ground, chiefly on social and economic grounds, Christianity apart.

(c) The Church as the whole Christ, members of the Body integrated into the Head (membra cum capite), is therefore, in our opinion, more likely to appeal to the true feelings of the African because the idea of Jesus Christ as the first-born among many brethren can readily be introduced in this context. Such an approach would be most effective in presenting the contrast between the ancestors to whom primacy in time is attributed, on the one hand, and Jesus Christ to whom we must unreservedly attribute a primacy in essence, on the other. This presentation is more germane to the earlier statement that in Jesus Christ we have the fundamental factor of perfect manhood associated with perfect godhead—two fundamentals without which the doctrine of the Incarnation is empty of all substance.

But here we have to be very cautious. Margaret Trowell, who, as an artist, has studied the African reaction to the Incarnation and the resultant expression of African understanding of this great mystery in artistic forms, has made the significant comment, "Few Africans would appear to have a mystical approach to religion. Their representation of the Christ was truly Very Man of Very Man, but failed completely to suggest Very God of Very God." She also says, "The idea of the Incarnation is not difficult for the African. In the pagan world, it happens on a lower level all the time. Every tree or stone, every snake or wild beast, may contain some spirit or other, and the gods and ancestors return to live again in whom they choose. No one knows clearly who may be so possessed, for it is not obvious to the casual observer. It is not obvious because the idea of moral value is not connected with the incarnate spirit. For the young African artist the idea of God incarnate is a perfectly natural conception. But although he knows theoretically that God—and therefore Christ—is perfect goodness, the idea that this quality should be visible in his painting is beyond him. His conception is inadequate and must surely grow, but even now he has perhaps something to teach us. Such a matter-of-fact acceptance of the immanence of God is surely a very real contribution to our doubting, puzzled world, even if it is an incomplete one."[54]

Margaret Trowell's comments are very instructive and deserve much careful consideration by all those who have a special interest in developing healthy theological concepts in the African Christian convert. Whilst we would defer to her specialist knowledge and comments as an artist, we would also note that writers like Parrinder, and Rattray before him, would not readily subscribe to the statement that "every tree or stone, every snake or wild beast, may contain some spirit or other . . ."[55] Certainly, the ancestors are not thought of as generally returning to live with whomsoever they choose. Among the Mende of Sierra Leone, for example, the spirit of a deceased child may be born more than once but by the same mother. The Yoruba postulate that grandparents are reincarnated in grandchildren born after their death and not in anyone per se.[56] The Akan also believe in reincarnation, but only within the maternal clan.[57]

(d) But the doctrine of the Incarnation also requires an associated doctrine of Jesus Christ as the messenger of God who sent out the early disciples to "Go forth and preach the Gospel to the whole world". This authority, we believe, has been handed down to the Church through its ministry. As Dr. Sundkler rightly observes, "To many an African pastor, the link of his Church with the Church of the Apostles will afford the guidance he needs in order to understand his own Ministry".[58] This notion, some of our readers might be tempted to say, is particularly non-Protestant and is true of the Orthodox, Roman

Catholic and some Anglicans. In fact, its author is a Swedish Lutheran Bishop. It is, however, most relevant to note that, in Africa, the skills associated with witch-doctors and the priests of many of the cults are either handed down from father to son or from master to pupil. The *Asantehene* is the example *par excellence*. He inherits the Golden Stool from his predecessor by a special rite of appointment and *de jure* becomes "King or Chief of the Priests".[59] He is thus "supreme priest of his country, for in his hands lies the cult of his departed ancestors and he represents the priests in the state council".[60] The implied doctrine of apostolic succession not only does not create any difficulty for Africans, but is part of their life-setting and thought-setting.

(e) Again, the concept of the Great Family needs to be bolstered up, particularly because of the rapid disruption of the traditional extended family engendered by the increasing industrialization projects all over Africa, the consequential development of new townships and the exodus from the villages. This widespread trend towards city life is naturally producing a large floating population of *déracinés*, who, having cut loose from their tribal environment, have also broken loose from the concomitant moral sanctions. Morality in the African community is linked up with religion, on the basis of *cujus regio hujus religio*; *cujus religio hujus consuetudo*, the last term embracing the various taboos and sanctions of the group. The Christian Church can, however, provide a fresh mould into which people from diverse areas and of varied environmental background may find a common unifying influence, in Jesus Christ who then becomes the first-born among many brethren, all of whom can find in Him a common bond of kinship.

In order to make explicit the nature of kinship in Christ, for Africans, let us take a brief look at kinship in the African situation. There are, in general, two distinct types: first, agnatic kinship which indeed controls degrees within which marriage contracts can be established, and, second, age-mate kinship which generates a bond of fellow-feeling between men and women contemporaries. In a discussion of the Church as a family, agnatic kinship systems are not relevant. But the age-mate kinships are greatly so. We recall that the several communities exist in a covenant-relation based on tribe, clan and family. Of these three, the tribe seems to provide the most suitable exemplar for these discussions. The tribe, subsuming the clan and the family, provides a unifying centre of recognizable and demonstrable influence among the members of the various constituent clans and families. In particular, it provides the opportunities, especially through the initiation societies, for the cultivation of the idea of the larger family unit which transcends the separate clans and individual extended families.

It is difficult for those who are not members of those societies to be sure of what goes on in them; and, where one is such, one is solemnly bound by oath never to reveal their secrets. But, judging from the various gleanings available, it seems that their *raison d'être* implies a death to the old life on being initiated, and a birth to a new life when the initiates are returned to society as fully-fledged adult members of their communities. This is a theological concept, even if not Christian. The initiate is generally taken to a clearing surrounded by thick forests or by tall savannah grass, away from the town or village—a setting which evokes fear. The main rite may be circumcision or clitoridectomy as among the Kikuyu, or a scarring of the body of men initiated into *Poro*, and scarring after clitoridectomy in the cases of women initiated into Sande, as among the Mende; or a scarring of the body only as in the case of the *Anyota* (the leopard society) of the Congo. Sometimes the initiates are taught the value of courage, and how to be worthy of the ancestors; they may have to face danger and encounter serious hazards, as in the case of *Anyota* initiation.[61] In other cases, long protracted dances are celebrated—all night as among the Kikuyu or the Malinke of the Republic of Guinea to prepare the candidates for the great day. Thus, Camara Laye tells of a dancing ceremony preceding the rite of circumcision which naturally produced a psychological condition designed perhaps to lead to the great moment when one feels fear but indeed is too afraid to shout.[62]

Lukamba, one of Colin Turnbull's characters, tells us that, before he was initiated into the *Anyota* cult, he was first beaten with a stick and told not to be affrighted in any situation; and then he was left in a forest clearing, alone late at night. Later, whilst in this lonely setting, he saw the figure of a leopard rustling in the long grass around him; he was actually attacked by the leopard which clawed him, whilst making the most fearful growls. He was afraid but dared not show his fear. As he lay on the ground in the grip of the leopard he felt himself "as if dead". Then the leopard stopped growling, the clawing came to an end, and he came to life; the operator removed the mask and turned out to be someone he knew. He gave him a long lesson on the history of his country; of the struggles of the ancestors to win and maintain it; of the need for the young men to learn *never* to fear anything if they are to be worthy of the tradition of the ancestors. Lukamba had been born again. But he had to go through the experience of death—better described as being face to face with death—to cultivate manly courage worthy of his ancestors.

Camara Laye tells of the gun-shots which announced the birth of the initiate—"that one more man, one more Malinke, had been born". The criterion of this birth is, again, courage. "Truly your son has been brave!" are the words shouted to the mother of the circumcised boy. In the case of circumcision rites, "the blood must flow", as Camara Laye tells us. This common, we might say *communal*, flow of blood naturally creates a strong bond of kinship.

So, as Colin Turnbull again tells us, Ibrahim, another of his characters, regretted that he had been moved from his community and circumcised when under an anaesthetic in a hospital, instead of being allowed to go through the tribal demands of facing the rite in cold blood and "sharing blood" with his brothers. He bemoaned the fact that he was never given the opportunity of experiencing "death" like his brothers, and so he never felt he belonged to his people and in particular to the ancestors. He would "never be able to see the *nkumbi*, and would never be able to be a man".[63]

The same principle of cultivating courage in the face of fear seems also true of the female initiatory rites of which clitoridectomy is the major part in many areas. According to Jomo Kenyatta, Kikuyu initiates are removed from the town or village into a secluded clearing. Early in the morning they are taken to a stream and made to stand waist-deep in the running water presumably to numb the genital organs. Then they are brought back to the site prepared for the operations. They are made to sit on a hide and an elder member sits behind the initiate she sponsors. Then they assume a posture appropriate for the easy performance of the operations. Each older woman holds her candidate from behind, her legs interwoven with hers, so as to keep her steady; then the operator appears, it seems with her face painted with white and black ochre, and rattles tied on to her legs. Expectancy naturally evokes fear. Then the sharp burn, and the operation is over. A woman is born. "She has been brave!" the female spectators cry. In cases where scarring follows later, the birth is only completed after the marks have been duly put on. Once more *communal* blood flows and the fellow-initiates form an age-mate group.

In some cases, the communal feeling is strengthened by a later rite which completes the ceremonies. Thus among the Mende of Sierra Leone, Sande girls, on the day before their *début*, eat a common meal of rice from a common bowl in the centre of which stands a phallic symbol. They eat around this object, half-timidly, because they are not sure of the full significance of the meal. Participants say it has a peculiar taste which seems to make one feel satiated after eating the first mouthful. Some of this may be sent home to prospective husbands. The meal seems to have a distinct fertility aspect because the initiates are guided, perhaps by association, to think *inter alia* of child-bearing and wife-hood. In spite of the pronounced peculiar taste, the meal is consumed and marks the end of the initiation ceremonies. Rebirth is complete. Henceforth, the initiates must eschew their childhood attitudes and interests. They have now graduated into adult life and must live up to the role of their new status and responsibilities.

A good instance of the dramatization of rebirth is found in the final stages of Kikuyu initiation ceremonies. All the initiates, boys and girls, in any one group, are first adopted by an elderly couple as children. Then six, or in cases where there has been an illness twelve, days after the respective surgical operations, the adopting parents simulate the birth of their new children. They first of all welcome the initiates into a hut where they are allowed to sit around. The door is shut and silence is maintained. The mother and father go into a room which is also shut. After a short period the mother utters groans of child-birth pains and the father gets up, runs out and calls for a midwife. Meanwhile a sheep would have been sacrificed and its entrails preserved. A midwife responds to the call and brings in the gut of the sheep and sets it on a hide where the mother would have been seated. Another woman comes in and cuts the gut. The boys emit the roar of a lion, the girls join in with an applauding shriek. The gut is then cut into a long ribbon, and the initiates stand in a cluster. The gut is tied round the group in such a way as to cover the navels of the initiates standing in the circumference of the circle. The midwife then comes along with a razor dipped in the sheep's blood, cuts the ribbon in two, thereby symbolizing the severance of the umbilical cord. The initiates have now been born again. The birth-pangs of the mother, the yell of the initiates (like baby's first cry) and the separation of the umbilical cord recapitulate the stages of a natural birth.

Among the Mende of Sierra Leone at about 4 a.m. on the day of the presentation of the initiates back to their parents, the *Poro* spirit "groans and sighs mournfully" around the town like a woman in labour, thus giving birth to the newly initiated. They are thus reborn.[64] The initiates have been born again together and for ever they remain united in one body, i.e., concorporate. This concorporateness is indeed a key element in the puberty initiation ceremonies, and, as we have noted, it is essentially based on a blood-covenant relation. Its religious significance is an aspect of the initiation ceremonies which the anthropologists do not seem to have grasped. Thus, for example, Bruno Bettelheim misses this element in an otherwise significant discussion of the meaning of initiation rites in his book *Symbolic Wounds*.[65] For our purposes, it is sufficient to note that in those cases where circumcision has become a part of the male initiation rites, the communal flow of blood binds the initiates into a blood-covenant group. We hold also that the same principle is present in the practice of clitoridectomy for females. We would, therefore, go on to say that the puberty initiation rites, even when circumcision or clitoridectomy is not practised, lead in every case to the establishment of a blood-covenant group.

One further point must here be mentioned, viz., that the blood shed at circumcision always flows on to the ground without any attempt to stop it immediately after the operation.[66] This aspect of the rite is understood by some to mean that the initiates thereby give their life to the earth. But, since the ancestors lie in the earth when buried, the life of the initiates is blended with that of the ancestors thus identifying them with the ancestors. Behind this attitude lies one of the major arguments against the alienation of land in West Africa. The living cannot be separated from that extended aspect of their life which is deposited in the soil of their homeland, i.e., the ancestral graves. Another aspect of the puberty initiation ceremonies is that the "newly born" are given special instruction—on the history of the tribe and its organization, for the boys, and on child-bearing, child-nurture and the elements of housewifery for the girls—instruction which is denied to the uninitiated. So they become *enlightened* by their new knowledge to lead adult lives worthy of their tribe or clan. Then they take oaths of secrecy, promising not to divulge to the uninitiated any of the information so received.

It is interesting to recall here that, among the Jews, the phrase "the blood of the covenant" always referred to the blood shed at circumcision.[67] The "P-writer plainly states that any male who has not kept this 'covenant in the flesh' is to be excluded from the Israelite community". Not to be circumcised is to violate the covenant, and to lose the divine promise.[68] The Rabbis also taught that "in order to secure a blessed immortality, a man must normally be a Jew, for Israel is the heir—or at least, by somewhat grudging concession, a circumcised proselyte". "The circumcised foreskin is normally the guarantee of entry" to Paradise. For "Isaac is said to sit constantly at the entrance of

Gehinnom to deliver all his descendants from entering there-in".[69] This passage is very reminiscent of the notion present among the Congolese that without going through the rite of circumcision one is not "fit to live" with the ancestors after death.

Again, although the ancestors are ordinarily thought of as "spirit", it is universally assumed that they reside in their graves. So when one visits the grave of an ancestor, one expects him to be able to hear any words addressed to them all. For example, due notice is given, usually six days in advance, before the Mende of Sierra Leone make the customary offering of cooked rice mixed with red (i.e., unburnt) palm-oil. This notice consists of a request that all the ancestors, apparently addressed through the deceased at whose graveside the words are spoken, should wait, on the appointed day, for their visitors, however late in the day their arrival may be. The words used run like this:

"Grandpa so and so, I have come to tell you (plural) that we (i.e., your children) are coming six days from today to offer you all red-palm-oil-rice. Please do not go out (from this place) on that day until after we have been, however high the sun may have risen. You all, please, stay and await our arrival."

This discussion of kinship in Africa provides us with a very significant concept on which African Christians could build the concept of the Church as the Great Family.

Chapter 4

SOUND DOCTRINAL TEACHING—II

THE DISCUSSION in the last section of the previous chapter has led us to the point where we can see the significance of the initiation rites as a factor in tribal life. Initiation is the basis of age-kinship and tribal-kinship. It thus provides an identification of the living with the dead. This societary bond is built around blood-shedding—a blood-covenant. Christians also belong to a corporate existence built upon the blood-covenant of Jesus Christ. By baptism we become buried into Christ's death and indeed go through an experience of mystical death. And once we go through it we become *enlightened*. We learn from the Procatechesis of Cyril of Jerusalem that candidates who were being prepared for baptism were told, "Thou art within the Church's nets, submit to be taken; flee not, for Jesus would secure thee, not to make thee die, but by death to make thee live. For thou must die and rise again. . . . Die then to thy sins and live to righteousness: yea from this day forth, live."[1] They were also taught to understand that the catechizing that was to follow was not to be divulged to a catechumen. "Tell nothing to a stranger," they were told. The instructor continues: "See thou let out nothing; not that the things spoken do not deserve telling, but the ear that hears does not deserve receiving. Thou thyself wast once a Catechumen, and then I told thee not what was coming. When thou hast by practice reached the height of what is taught thee, then wilt thou understand that the Catechumens are unworthy to hear them."[2] "You who have been enrolled, are become the sons and daughters of one Mother . . ."[3] i.e., the Church.

The Christian notebook contains the essence of the basis of

the African initiation rites. The African initiate is told that he must die to his or her early life, but he must yield to the genius of the cult to live to the tribe. He or she becomes enlightened on learning the lore of the tribe; but this is secret, never to be revealed to anyone who has not yet been initiated. Like the age-groups of the African societies the Christians enrolled on any one baptismal occasion "become the sons and daughters" of one Mother. What more does the Christian Church in Africa need than to go back to the Church of the fourth century to find usages which can displace the pagan African customs and attitudes?

Again, the African community embraces the living, the unborn and the dead. Christians know of the Church militant, on earth, the Church triumphant, in heaven, and the Church expectant, in a state between the first two. In the Canon of the Mass they pray at the *Memento Domine*, that God may "grant some part and fellowship with Thy Holy Apostles and Martyrs ... into whose company we beseech Thee to admit us. ..."[4] This argument may be extended by two further stages. First, because Christians have entered into a mystical relation with Christ, they are exhorted to live "as those risen from the dead" (Romans 6: 13). This exhortation is a corollary of the fact that at baptism they are raised (from the dead by the Holy Spirit) to walk in newness of life. Second, in this resurrection life, they could attain the state of oneness (*henosis*) with Christ in which they could say like St. Paul:

> "I have been crucified with Christ: the life I now live is not my life, but the life which Christ lives in me; and my present bodily life is lived by faith in the Son of God, who loved me and sacrificed himself for me ..." (Gal. 2: 20 f., N.E.B.)

Here, the Christian is in *symbiosis* with Jesus Christ our elder brother, the first-born of many brethren. Unlike the ancestral dead of the Africans, Jesus Christ, once dead, *now lives*. Every true Christian has a personal experience of Him as a life-giving Spirit, returned to His place of glory in the Godhead. He also knows from the testimony of the Bible that Jesus Christ was seen after His resurrection by up to five hundred brethren (1 Cor. 15: 6, cf. Acts 10: 40 ff.).

Africans, on the other hand, whilst claiming that their ancestors are alive in the spirit do so without any concrete evidence. This belief in their existence is based primarily on dreams and not on any empirical or theological grounds. (We may here observe that dreams, so far as we can tell, are purely subconscious commentaries on the dreamers.) But these dreams determine the life of the people who behave according to the dictates of those as it were risen from the dead. The day-to-day life is, accordingly, so ordered as to please the ancestors. Disasters and illnesses are attributed to their anger, and success in one's undertakings is the outcome of their approval, and, therefore, of their blessing. The ancestors thus come to be regarded as the co-guardians with the cultic spirits of the *mores* of the community. Dr. Baeta succinctly states this relationship, when he said at a United Christian Council Conference in Accra in 1955, ". . . whatever others may do in their own countries, our people live with their dead".[5]

All of us Africans feel that our deceased parents and other ancestors are close to us. In the present context, therefore, Christian doctrinal teaching should be directed towards, first, presenting the Church as a corporate body with a unique solidarity transcending by far anything akin to it in pagan African society; and, second, discovering a means of preserving the tribe, solidarity of living and dead, as Africans understand that relationship, but in a new idiom, that of the community of the Church. In any case, ancestors are thought of in relation to their tribes or clans or families. They could, therefore, be readily embraced within the framework of the universal Church and be included within the communion of saints.

This suggestion poses *in se* an important theological problem in view of the fact that Christian prayers are said on behalf of "the faithful departed". Non-Christians are thus excluded. We would, however, ask: Is there no room for including non-Christians in our prayers? We do so for the living; as for example, when we pray for the peace of the world. Is it wrong then, to do the same for the dead? Our interpretation of the feeling of Christians of New Testament times leads us to the conclusion that they had a real concern for their relatives and compatriots who had died either before the establishment of the Christian Church (in the case of non-Christians) or before the Parousia (in the case of Christians). In particular, we would mention the Matthean record that at the death of Jesus Christ, "many of God's people arose from sleep and coming out of their graves after his resurrection they entered the Holy City, where many saw them" (Mt. 27: 52 f., N.E.B.). Other such references are to the "baptism for the dead" (1 Cor. 15: 29), the *descensus ad inferos* (1 Pet. 3: 18) and to the dead in Christ rising at the Parousia (1 Thess. 4: 14–18).

But, perhaps more significant than this concern, is the inclusion by the writer of the Epistle to the Hebrews in "his roll of heroes", of figures of the past, "some whom he himself must have recognized as being very imperfect specimens of humanity . . .", like Gideon, Samson and Barak, whom C. H. Dodd describes as being "no better than savages". We would add Rahab, the prostitute, to Dodd's list. Dodd goes on to say, "Their presence in any Christian 'heaven' is incongruous enough"; but he also recognizes that "upon the faith and courage of just such primitive ancestors our later achievements rest. They were not perfect, it is true; without us they could not be made perfect. But in the deathless society of the people of God they draw upon the treasury of life to which more enlightened generations have since contributed their experience of the love of God."[6]

We suggest that Dodd's language is eminently applicable to the African situation in view of the covenant relationship which we described earlier. If the African *lives* with his dead, he would naturally feel himself in the wrong place if there was no opportunity for him to realize the hoped-for comradeship with his ancestors, just because he had become a Christian.[7] We would, therefore, go on to suggest that the prayers of African Christians might in the providence of God lead to the salvation of their pagan ancestors. Indeed, we may justifiably add that it is highly probable that some of the dead for whom the early Christians were baptized had never heard of the promise of salvation through Jesus Christ. At best, they had not responded to the preaching of the Gospel even if they had heard it. How often do we not feel that if some of the current drugs—penicillin, aureomycetin, and Salk vaccine, for example—had been discovered, say, fifty years ago, some of our relatives might not have died when they did. We are inclined to the view that just as the progress of medicine has been influenced by the fatality caused by certain diseases to our predecessors, so, in the context of the saving work of Jesus Christ, God in His wisdom may have "made a better plan, that only in company with us should they reach their perfection" (Heb. 11: 40, N.E.B.). "For in Christ there is renovation and fulfilment, not only of sanctified persons, but also of the whole creation; and this transformation takes place within a new world-order whose outward form is vitally significant since it manifests the new organism of Christ."[8]

The *Watu wa Mngu*, one of the new religions of the Gikuyu (Kikuyu), adopt the Christian practice of venerating the saints in the belief that their ancestral spirits would act effectively in interceding to God on their behalf; ". . . by following the ancestral line, the spirits of the Gikuyu ancestors, who had departed before the coming of Christianity, would thereby profit by the transaction, for in providing for the welfare of their descendants they would find the opportunity of maintaining their contact with the earth".[9] We would say that by praying for the unconverted ancestral dead we may help them to discover the love of God, wherever they may be, and in doing so find the means of attaining eternal salvation.

It is significant that although the Society for the Propagation of the Gospel commenced work in the Gold Coast (now Ghana) in 1751, and the Methodists in 1830, with various other Christian bodies like the Basel Mission following later,[10] Dr. K. Busia, himself a practising Methodist, could still say, in 1955, before the United Christian Council of the Gold Coast, that Christianity had been and was likely to remain "an alien and superficial addition to more hospitable creeds".[11] It is equally remarkable that Dr. Baeta, speaking at the same conference after Dr. Busia did not rebut this statement. Of course, he did make a defence of the Christian Church against what he termed "the quite generally held view that Christianity has not struck any very deep roots here" (i.e., Ghana).[12] Dr. Busia was thinking of the receptivity of Ashanti religiousness which had enabled them to embrace "the beliefs and the rites of conquered as well as of neighbouring tribes".[13] If this hospitality were adopted by Christians, it could readily lead to a syncretism of Christianity and pagan beliefs. We must therefore distinguish between the easy amalgamation of the Ashanti creeds with other foreign creeds and the incompatibility of Christianity with the nature religions.

A careful reading of Dr. Baeta's book, *Prophetism in Ghana*, leads us to the conclusion that the "spiritual" churches which he has studied are an amalgam of Christianity with Judaism and not a syncretism of Christianity with the nature religions of Ghana. We are struck by their *resistance* to "ancestor worship" and "fetish" and "juju" practices;[14] their adoption of the Levitical purificatory regulations concerning women, and polygamy;[15] their belief that the Old and New Testaments are of equal weight; their attachment to the Ark;[16] their retention of the Bible[17] and of some prayers of the historic churches.[18] It is, of course, true that the "spiritual" Churches emphasize healing and divination. But the recorded divination of one such Church from outside Ghana is quite instructive. We give here a sample of seven divinations separately given to a number of male enquirers. The date is June 7, 1947. Cryptic sounds, made up of agglomerations of letters, preface and end each oracle.

(1) Mr. A.

"For complete seven days, see to it that you are always the last to leave the house of prayer.

I will create in thee a new Zion and I will build for thee a strong tower."

"Fear not, neither be thou dismayed because I am with you to guide you in all your ways, saith the Lord. No hair of your head will fall down to the ground. Many oppose you; many will vie with you, but you can hold firm to the end. I shall increase and bless you as Joseph. Set apart three days; fast and pray for steadfastness and I will grant unto you joy and glory."

(2) Mr. B.

"Your fastings are not in vain, your struggles are not without effect; wait patiently to see the reward of your labour because when the wicked is cut off from the land, the righteous will gain and inherit it."

"There are two trials more for you before the year ends but if you overcome you will gain three blessings. Mr. B, loose not your girdle till the month of October is past, because you will have to battle within and without. Pray to conquer false accusation in the office. Pray to conquer bad neighbours. Pray to defeat sickness over your family. I will send you help; but love all, trust few, rely on Jesus as your best guide and surely it will be good for you.

"The Lord said, from November onwards things will change for the better and you will go on from joy unto joy, said the Lord Almighty.

"Never you be a doubter. I have called you to labour and I will uphold thee to the end."

(3) Mr. C.

"Thou art mine; for seven days completely, thou shalt be in my house and for this period shalt thou keep watch in my temple; sleep there, pray there and watch for me said the Lord. I shall reveal unto you great and mighty things. I shall reveal unto you several things. Be thou steadfast for there is much for thee to do for me."

"I have a need of you here,* in Gambia and in Gold Coast. There is great need of you overseas and I will bless you much in the ministry. Steer clear from all worldliness; counsel not with the body because you will be a mighty man before me."

"The Lord said, you are quenching the spirit of God,

* i.e., Sierra Leone.

deliver my messages and ask for more power because I will
be with thee."

(4) Mr. D.

"The Lord said, D will come back, if not in health, he will
come back in sickness; within the next months he will
declare my wondrous works."

"Where can he go? Where could he hide? His own
trouble is slight. Ollabbeffummottawwee is his star for if he
refuses my friendly call, three special dogs will drive him
here."

(5) Mr. E.

"Confess your sins boldly because you have sinned before
me. The Lord said, there is a great temptation in your venture; but if both of you could pray, fast and be steadfast,
there will be victory at the end. You are scattering too much.
Pray fervently."

(6) Mr. F.

"You need to pray for constancy and firmness of opinion;
you need also to be careful of under-estimating the power of
God in you, thereby permitting the devil to strangle your
efforts through fears and doubts. The Lord said unto me,
your mother is still alive and she thinks of you, help her by
your prayers. Your trials and temptations are in persistency,
fear and doubts, thoughts of evil happening or pessimism.
Pray unto God to give you patience, sense and wisdom. You
will do much to uphold the fort, said the Lord. Counsel not
with evil; don't be easily led by evil advisers; during the
months of June to August, I will come unto thee with new
powers and mighty revelations. Fast and don't be lazy to
pray."

(7) Mr. G.

"Thou art mine, I have called thee, doubt no more. I have
given you victory over three deaths; rejoice and be happy.
Thus said the Lord, you will not suffer hunger or thirst. Let

your whole aim always be to do your best daily in helping others. I will provide for you. Thus said the Lord, you are to wash in a brook or flowing water for seven days and some signs of illness will be washed away from you—quench not my spirit. Avoid all tale-bearers; join no one to speak or say evil. Avoid any gift of food now because of poison and illness. If you will struggle on, you will gain the key of tongues that you have carelessly missed."

The diagnoses of the troubles of the enquirers are, as may be seen, invariably a lack of a firm faith in God. The correctives suggested are prayer, fasting and a firm faith, with a promise of power to serve God better in some cases. It is remarkable that in twenty such divinations which we have studied, some dated June 1947 and others June 1949, a firm faith in God, the power of God and prayer, are prominent; four counsel against the temptations of women. The fear of witches and poison is dispelled by the promise of God's protection to all who believe in Him. In several cases God promises to make the enquirers powerful evangelists.

But perhaps the best illustration from Africa of the resistance of Christianity to pagan rites is to be found in the opposition of Ashanti Christians, in the 1940s, to the authority of the Ashanti chiefs. Dr. Busia tells us that Ashanti Christians, Roman and non-Roman, objected to actions ranging from "swearing an oath in the traditional way, providing sheep for sacrifice at the hearing of a case, carrying a stool or sword on ceremonial occasions, to doing communal labour on the road".

The resistance crystallized in 1942 with the refusal of Christians to observe Thursday as a day of rest. "The Ashanti Confederacy Council of Chiefs" had ruled that there should be a relation between every Ashanti and the fifth day of the week, Thursday, the natal day of the Earth Goddess, *Asaase Yaa*. Representatives of the Churches contended that the only appropriate authority to legislate for them on religious matters was the Church, which had already established a ritual relation between Christians and the first day of the week. They appealed to the *Asantehene* and the Chief Commissioner. The deadlock was fortunately resolved by the Chief Commissioner who refused to sanction "the order of the Confederacy Council".[19] Dr. Busia did not, however, indicate how far the rank and file of the Churches participated in the resistance to the Thursday regulation. Did the ordinary Christian feel he did not wish to conform to the demands of the Confederacy?

As far as the ancestral sacrificial rites were concerned, Dr. Busia tells us that "literates and illiterates, Christians and pagans, have participated in ritual *Adae* ceremonies", and that, on questioning the young men, "literate and Christian", who have been privileged to attend the pouring of the libations to ancestors, or have witnessed the sacrifices at *Adae* and similar ceremonies, "in many instances their answers were, 'I felt its reality', or 'I was deeply moved'—implying a very exalted feeling of awe". He wrote this account in 1951. Surely the virility implied in the resistance to *Asaase Yaa* should have induced a strong reaction against these rites, had the ordinary Christian in the pew possessed it.

Worse still, on March 7, 1957, the Ga tribal officials, in whose area Accra is situated, organized a public libation ceremony to mark the Independence of Ghana. Once again, leaders of the Churches, we gather, left the arena in which the celebrations were held, in protest; but the average Ghanaian present stayed on. The sequel was a long series of newspaper articles on the propriety of libations. Today, libations are publicly poured to the ancestors by Ghanaians, whether "literate and Christian", or not. Indeed, J. H. Nketia of Ghana has observed, "In Ghana, popular imagination has seized upon libation as a possible contribution which African worship can offer to the Christian Church. Libation is interpreted by many educated Christians as a concrete method of prayer which they consider ritually satisfying and helpful in the concentration of their faculties."[20] Dr. Busia also says, "The ceremonialism connected with ancestor worship has made it a resilient force which Christianity has not assailed".[21] Pluralism threatens to stand firm, and the Church must seek to find an appropriate answer.

We think that such an answer will best be given in terms of

the great family founded in Jesus Christ, with a real concern for the ancestral dead who may not even have been Christians during their lifetime. Judging from the prayers offered, libation ceremonies seem to persist because they maintain the social values engendered by regard for the ancestors and the continuance of the race. If God is represented as He from whom all fatherhood in heaven and on earth is named, Christians are those who are concorporate with Christ. We must also add here that God intends to "sum up all things in Christ" (Eph. 1: 10). He is therefore potentially the Father of the ancestral dead. The Christian practice of venerating the saints is based on their membership within the great Christian family.

In this fact of the great Christian family lies the theological answer which pagan Africans do not understand, and which justifies the Christian belief in the existence of the spirits of the faithful departed. Orthodox Christians may find that, in assuming the possibility of a conversion to the love of God in Christ beyond the grave, this offering of libations may give way to prayers being offered on behalf of the beloved dead. If we, as Christians, have been adopted into Sonship by God, then we have a stronger case than the pagan African for believing that God our Father is indeed our Ancestor.

Christians have a further argument in their favour. Dr. J. B. Danquah asserts that the Akan have a "revealed" Messiah, *Nana*. The Akan Messiah is a human king, "the anointed of the Akan people" who was "produced, invented, fashioned or hewed out by his community". He had lived the life of one fit to rule and lead his people as "head of the family, chief of the tribe, patriarch of the clan or king of the State". In this position "he had been anointed and had, in addition, been worshipped with acts of adoration and reverence as someone like a god, or one who was about to become a god". This revelation was complete at the death of the ruler, *Opanyim*, when he was deified and became *Nana*. For Dr. Danquah, the Akan concept of a Messiah is best expressed by a maxim which, when translated into English, reads: "A thing of dishonour and a son of the Akan go ill together".[22]

This conception of the Messiah is utterly different from that of Christians. It is a process. The Christian Church in its wisdom long ago rejected the suggestion that Jesus Christ advanced from pure manhood into the Godhead. This was the heresy canvassed in the third century A.D. by Paul of Samosata.[23] Nor do we claim that the Messiah was "produced", "invented" or fashioned by men. Our interpretation of the Godhead leads us to recognize a Trinity of Persons, distinct in their functions as Father, Son and Holy Spirit. Of these, the Messiah is the Son of God, Himself God from before the foundation of the world, but not Father. He is the agent of Creation and enjoys a cosmic lordship of the universe. And so the Incarnation was a *descensus ad terram*, which St. Paul beautifully describes in Phil. 2: 5 ff.

"For the divine nature was his from the first; yet he did not think to snatch at equality with God, but made himself nothing, assuming the nature of a slave. Bearing the human likeness, revealed in human shape, he humbled himself, and in obedience accepted even death—death on a Cross". (N.E.B.)

The Christian Messiah is thus the converse of the Akan Messiah. The latter is first a ruler—a human ruler—whom men venerate; who, when he has been enstooled as ruler, *Opanyim*, must not touch the ground or else he would be desecrated, and who is kept away from the presence of death or any influence which it is believed may be death-radiating. He does die, as is natural, and only then is deity conferred on him by his subjects. The Christian Messiah, on the other hand, first possessing deity, assumed humanity, and of course "increased in wisdom and stature and in favour with God and men" (Luke 2: 52, R.S.V.). We note the favour our Lord found was not only with men, but is significantly described by the third Evangelist as first "with God". In His incarnate existence, He did not avoid death. He touched the bier containing the corpse of the young man of Nain, and restored him to life (Luke 7: 11-17). He went to Lazarus' grave and raised him from the dead (John 11: 1-53). Instead of being waited upon like an Akan *Nana*, He washed His disciples' feet

(John 13: 12–16) to give them an example of humble service, and openly asserted that the "Son of Man came not to be ministered unto, but to minister and give His life a ransom for many" (Mark 10: 45). His whole life was one of voluntary self-abasement in order to make human beings rich (2 Cor. 8: 9).

Again, the deity attained by the Akan *Nana* is a personal status. The *Opanyim* may, as a human ruler, have been a bene-factor; but as *Nana*, i.e., in his deified state, he has not conferred any extra benefits on his people. The Christian Messiah, on the other hand, brought salvation from God to man. He, by His resurrection from the dead, provided mankind with the guaran-tee of their own resurrection. Indeed, as a result of the incarna-tion, human nature was taken up into the Godhead, and Chris-tians have come to realize that their God knows from experience what suffering is. Dr. Danquah calls his Akan Messiah the "nearest-to-God man", a phrase which is reminiscent of the Christian Messiah; but he makes no reference to that Messiah being good and not avoiding disgrace. In other words, the Akan criteria for Messiahship are purely human. We, on the other hand, maintain that Jesus Christ was good and lived a sinless life because, and only because, His will was conterminous with the will of God. Again, Dr. Danquah develops a recurrent series of human Messiahs, later deified, from which he infers the value of a universal *Nana*.[24] For the Christian, the Messiah is Himself *universal*, exercising cosmic sovereignty over all things, including death (Col. 1: 15–20; 1 Cor. 15: 24–27).

Since the Akan *Nana* is, in fact, a human father to his subjects, then his deification represents a human attempt to give a concrete demonstrable content to the conception of deity. At the same time he is an inaccessible father who can only be approached, much of the time, through a spokesman, the *Ɔkyeame*. So he is not in direct contact with his people. The Christian position is different. The Christ is He who became man and lived as man. His life is an inspiration for all time—in a truly spiritual sense, and for sinners only—not for the man of exceptional virtue.* He

* The basic notion on which the New Testament establishes man's

first provides us with a concrete demonstrable manifestation of deity and also becomes the bridge-head by which we may gain access to God the Father. So He is the first-born among many brethren and as elder brother we have direct and complete access to him. But because He is universal, He provides the meeting-ground of all Christians, whether Jew or Greek, African or Chinese, slaves or freemen, male or female. We thus become co-heirs of the Kingdom of God with Him (cf. Romans 8: 16 f., 29; Gal. 3: 27 ff.; Eph. 2: 11–22, 3: 6 f.; 1 Pet. 2: 9 f.; Mt. 8: 11). This universal meeting ground is not provided by the Akan Messiah.

We may, therefore, go on to state that the Christian Messiah satisfies a wider range of situations than anything postulated of the Akan Messiah. In particular, the Christian Messiah is not just a distant head of a family that venerates but has no direct access to Him; He is indeed the leader of the family as the first-born of the family line. In the African situation we can make one further point. The primary criterion of membership within the family is the *mother*. So, in Ghana, succession was determined matrilineally. A man's heir was his sister's son because although his own son inherited his *sunsum*, or, later, his *ntorɔ*, and not the mother's, yet the blood on which his nephew was fed in the foetus came from a woman who had shared common foetal blood with him. Thus, the Akan say that one can always be sure of one's mother but one may have a putative father. So, too, among the Mende of Sierra Leone, a man may marry the daughter of his mother's brother by the same father, but not his father's sister's daughter. The guiding principle here is that, in the former case but not in the latter, the two children share foetal blood with their parents.

In the language of Christian theology the Church is the mother of all Christians, but the Church owes its origin to Jesus Christ, whose Body it is. Therefore membership of the family of the Church brings us into a foetal bond based on Jesus Christ.

---

salvation through the death of Christ is that "all men are sinners without any exception" (cf. Mk. 2: 17, Lk. 15: 11–32, *imp.* v. 32; 18: 9–14; Romans 3: 23, 5: 8, 13).

Accordingly, that family is based on a surer foundation than one that is centred around a common father. In situations where monogamy has prevailed, confident conjugal loyalty has removed any suggestion of a putative father and therefore succession becomes unquestionably patrilineal. The New Testament, stressing monogamy as it does, affords Christians the guarantee of true membership of one family, the great family of the Church. The polygamous *Opanyim*, later deified as *Nana*, has no such undisputed family and is therefore not an appropriate rallying ground for his own children.

The Christian family, because it is centred around Jesus Christ, enjoys the benefits available in the Holy Spirit. St. Paul tells us in 1 Cor. 12: 12 f., that we are all irrigated by the Holy Spirit at baptism, and later declares in 2 Cor. 1: 21 that we are all anointed by God. This means that the co-heirship we enjoy in Christ is tantamount to a co-anointing with Him. Because of this, the grace of Jesus Christ described in 2 Cor. 8: 9 inspires in us a "grace" which seeks to maintain the well-being of our fellow-members in the Body of Christ. So St. Paul, writing to the Corinthians, stresses that the spiritually rich must seek to share their spiritual endowments with those who lack them, and those who have material blessings must give of their bounty to those who need them—so as to produce an equality of possessions. This equalization of possessions is, however, based on the strengthening of certain virtues: "faith", "utterance", "knowledge", "earnestness" and "love" towards the apostles (2 Cor. 8: 7). What better catalogue can one find in seeking to build up a well-founded family?

We would conclude by saying that the great family of the Church established in Jesus Christ and by Him provides all the answers for a sound healthy community of persons. Anointed with the Holy Spirit they all share in common the Holy Spirit of God the Father, and are nourished by the one mother, the Church, with Jesus Christ as the uniting factor (cf. 1 Cor. 12: 12).

Lastly we must note that the *Opanyim* is purely a type of the universal *Nana* and not that *Nana* himself. We Christians believe that the Godhead is indivisible. Where Christ is, there God is. Accordingly, Christ represents the love of God for man in concrete form; He is not merely a limited version of the possibilities of Godhead. Indeed, it was whilst we were still hostile in our attitude to God that Jesus Christ came to die for us to reconcile us to God (cf. Romans 5: 8 ff.; 2 Cor. 5: 19). It is, therefore, a matter of prime importance that "the status of Jesus amongst the ancestors and other spirits" be made distinctly clear to African converts to Christianity.[25] We must go on to enquire into the nature of immortality.

THE DOCTRINE OF IMMORTALITY

This doctrine is inadequately understood and not too well discussed in the standard books on the theme. In general, primary emphasis seems to be laid on the difference between the Greek concept of the immortality of the soul *per naturam* and the fact that in Christian thought "eternal life" is the gift of God. The Greek position postulates that the soul will continue to live on after death, and, if it had acquired the necessary intellectual start in this life, it would continue to make progress in the life after death. The African position, though not stressing progress in the other world, does imply a survival which seems to be analogous to the Greek concept. Most African groups believe, as we have already noted, that the soul (spirit) of an individual exists in some form with the same passions as he had when alive. The practice, in some areas, of making sure that a person is duly buried is based on this assumption. In contrast, the corpse of a witch is either dismembered, as by the Temne of Sierra Leone, or burned, as by the Efik of Calabar, or thrown to the hyaenas, as among some tribes in Nyasaland, because he is not to be "permitted to survive death". Among the Kikuyu, if a man was convicted of practising *Orogi*, i.e., by poisoning a man, a woman, or child, "he was accused of witchcraft, tried and, if found guilty, burnt up".

Christian theologians have so far omitted any important discussion on survival after death, and have quite rightly emphasized the doctrine of resurrection and, with it, the question of "eternal life". But resurrection is in fact a complex notion, partly experienced in this life by all those who are baptized into the Body of Christ, and fully realized after death. At the same time, resurrection implies the death of body, soul and spirit and their later revival by the power of the Holy Spirit. This suggests that when we talk of resurrection we mean the quickening of the whole personality of the individual.

But here we are confronted with serious questions: (a) What is the meaning of death? (b) If the Christian notion of resurrection is maintained, are we to go on to say that the soul, or the spirit, of an individual dies as well as the body; if so does the soul or the spirit die in the same way as the body does? (c) How are the various answers to the foregoing questions related to the doctrine of "eternal death"? How indeed are we to understand the Pauline dictum that "the wages of sin is death" (Rom. 6: 23)? Questions like these demand serious consideration if Christian theologians hope to convince African converts to Christianity that there will be a final resurrection of the dead and that God will clothe the resurrected person with a spiritual body, as we learn in 1 Corinthians.

Alongside all this is the question of the Church expectant and the Church triumphant. In which of these categories can we place the dead ancestors? More pertinent still is the mediaeval conception of purgatory and hell. One would hope that the problem of a conversion to Christ after death would be examined side by side with the discussion of "eternal death". Subsequent to all these questions will arise that which concerns all Africans, viz.: What is the role of the spirits of the ancestors? Do they really provide us with material benefits, or can we rightly say that their usefulness lies in a mediatorial role of prayer to God on our behalf?

Christians, must, of course, reject the suggestion among Africans that the dead maintain, in a spiritual condition, the interests and concerns, the passions and joys, which they had in their physical existence. At the same time, it is true that *homo sapiens* has through the centuries (one million years ?) developed a personality, by a long and painful process in the upward path from his co-primates to "manhood". The average span of human life is, however, so short that invariably man dies just when he can demonstrate the "promise and potency" of new development. Even the most mature men display at the time of their death the promise of still greater maturity and richer wisdom. Is it, therefore, not reasonable to suppose that "in a rational universe", human personality is not pointlessly destroyed by physical death?

"If we once reach the conviction that personality is undestroyed by physical death", writes Professor Wheeler Robinson, "then we have already in personality the content of a life beyond death, or the beginning of such a content."[26]

Personality, as we know it, is never ready-made at birth. It always needs a social environment to nourish and cherish it. It is the product of the impact of the social community to which the individual belongs and his innate potentialities. C. H. Dodd, observing that the societary influence often fails to produce the expected results, makes the comment, relevant to this discussion, that these "failures are not final, if it be true that the family of God on earth and heaven is one, and that the sharing of life crosses the barrier of death".[27] This interpretation of the state of the dead is not based on their mere survival, but on their attaining a new organic existence, brought into being and enriched by the love of God. This is immortality.

We would further add that African communities assume that the ancestors go to a place after they die. The Mende say the good man goes to *Dadagolehun* or *Ŋanyagolehun*, the country of "white sand". The Yoruba say they go to *Orun*, variously called *Orun Rere*, *Orun Funfun*, *Orun Baba Emi*—"Good *Orun*", "White *Orun*", "Our Father's *Orun*".[28] The Akan postulate an "Upper Kingdom—the confederation of the heavenly bodies, the sun, moon and stars", to which the *kra* of a dead man first goes before making its way to the City of Nyankopon, "which is on the sun" where it first greets "the Royal Ancestors, who as representatives of *Nyankopon*, the Sun-god, rule the heavenly kingdom for him". Then, after appearing before a court of judgment, the *kra* of a good man goes to "settle on the planet from which he received it at his birth".[29] All three instances we have quoted imply a paradisical existence for the good.

If the Christian teaching is to make immortality clear these notions must be corrected. Does the good man go direct to heaven as Protestant theology asserts, or does everybody—good and bad alike—go through a preliminary purgation? The language of Luke 12: 58 f. suggests that "the sinner can expiate his sin in Sheol and so escape Gehenna".[30] For Catholic Christians, purgatory is an accepted presupposition.

Without admitting all the implications of Roman Catholic teaching on this subject, we recognize the basic logic inherent in the concept. At least we would propose a plea for accepting the notion of a preliminary period of purgation before man attains the "beatific vision", during which the dead are purged of "whatever defilements they may have contracted in the midst of this miserable and naughty world, through the lusts of the flesh or the wiles of Satan", so that "they may be presented pure and without spot before God".[31] Modern Lutheran theologians are beginning to see the relevance of this notion in discussions of the state of the dead. One writer, Martensen, sets out a non-Roman Catholic attitude eminently well when he says,

> "as no soul leaves this present existence in a fully complete and prepared state, we must suppose that there is an intermediate state, a realm of progressive development in which souls are prepared and matured for the final judgment. Though the Romish doctrine of Purgatory is repudiated because it is mixed up with so many crude and false positions, it nevertheless contains the truth that the intermediate state must in a purely spiritual sense be a purgatory designed for the purifying of the soul."[32]

Since ancestor worship has proved to be a vital influence in African society, because it maintains a fellowship between the living and the dead, we would, with Wheeler Robinson, postulate the enrichment of this fellowship by making the Christian religion the middle term between the personality and the life beyond the grave. For Christians, this is fellowship with God. Ancestor worship never seems to rise to this height. God has no place in ancestor worship *in se*. The ancestors are generally requested to "make the earth fruitful, the women bear children, the children grow up sturdy in body, and the men successful in their undertakings". It is based on the tribal or clan or family covenant relationship. But it knows no fellowship between the living and the dead.

Christian teaching, based on the Incarnation, might then, first of all, state that God intends man to be in fellowship with Him (Eph. 2: 16, 18), and that, through this fellowship with God, we are led into a new fellowship with our fellow-men (Eph. 3: 6); in other words, that the Incarnation provides the basis for a common life. We can then venerate the ancestors, but not pour libations to them. We may then rightly pray for their souls, and, if we are prepared to accept that their personalities do not perish with death, expect them to feel a concern for us and make intercession to God for us. This interpretation of the state of the ancestral dead would readily dispose of the belief in reincarnation, because Christian teaching allows for a resurrection life, imparted by God, which admits of the preservation of man's individuality, and rejects any suggestion either of his absorption into the Alone, as the Gnostics and Hindus suggest, or of his return to the "unformed mass of the race" according to the Akan.[33] But this resurrection life is based on the resurrection life of Jesus Christ whom God raised from the dead. His resurrection is the guarantee of ours (1 Cor. 15: 12–29). But it begins here and now under the influence of the Holy Spirit. So St. Paul can say to the Roman Christians, "The body is dead because of sin; but the Spirit is life because of righteousness" (Romans 8: 10 f.).

The human spirit infused with the life-giving Spirit of God through baptism assumes the quality we call eternal life. Such a spirit, when the body passes through the experience of physical death, must preserve its capacity to endure. St. Paul also adds the further note that when God's Holy Spirit possesses any man He will quicken his mortal body. Some may object, and perhaps rightly so, that this discussion is primarily relevant to the man who in this life accepts Jesus Christ as Lord and Saviour. But, once again, we must not predetermine God's attitude to non-Christians. We may rightly and in all humility postulate that, on the final day of Judgment, God "shall be all in all", and pray that all men may have come to grasp His unspeakable love.[34] This last comment, however, calls for a brief discussion of the omnipotence of God.

The Doctrine of the Omnipotence of God

The concept of the omnipotence of God, as Christians understand it, stems from the Old Testament concept of God as being the Author of history. He created the world and orders it. In particular, He chose Abraham and created from his descendants the chosen race of Israel, manifesting His power in the exodus and the settlement in Canaan and subsequently in the return from the exile about five hundred years afterwards. He thus proved Himself superior to Chemosh and Melkart and all the lesser deities of Canaan. He destroyed Pharaoh, Sisera and their hosts. With His omnipotence were associated His glory, creation, and the moral qualities of justice, integrity and reliability, which were manifested in the covenant relation which He established between Himself and Israel (Ps. 136). But this special privilege which Israel came to enjoy through their election came to be interpreted to mean that God was always on the side of the righteous man and the righteous nation; the righteous nation would not be utterly destroyed by superior hostile forces from a heathen country, and the righteous man was never forsaken nor would his children ever be so poverty-stricken as to have to beg their bread. God might punish them when they forsook His ways, but His love was never in question; so He was always ready to restore them whenever they repented. The unrighteous man, however, He destroyed, although, as in the case of Israel, He did restore the repentant apostate into His good grace later on, as we see in the story of the exile. One is tempted to suggest that, for the average Hebrew, the sum total of his religion may be summarized in the words of Psalm 144: 11-15,

> Rescue me from the cruel sword,
> and deliver me from the hand of aliens,
> whose mouths speak lies,
> and whose right hand is a right hand of falsehood.
> May our sons in their youth
> be like plants full grown,
> our daughters like corner pillars
> cut for the structure of a palace;
> may our garners be full,
> providing all manner of store;
> may our sheep bring forth thousands
> and ten thousands in our fields;
> may our cattle be heavy with young,
> suffering no mischance or failure in bearing;
> may there be no cry of distress in our streets!
> Happy the people to whom such blessings fall!
> Happy the people whose God is the Lord! (R.S.V.)

On the whole, the prevalent teaching of the Old Testament presents God as always being on the side of the good man. Indeed, even when the wicked man achieves material prosperity his success is portrayed as running along a slippery path, leading him later on to total and complete destruction. God never justified the ungodly (Ex. 23: 7; Ps. 37, 13). The later notions of the arrival of a Messiah and the resurrection of the dead are intimately related to the ultimate glorification of the righteous and the destruction of the wicked on the day when God's glory shall be fully manifested on earth. On the other hand, when we study the New Testament we find there a different climate of opinion.

We would venture to suggest that the breach is widest between the Old and the New Testaments in the context of the omnipotence of God.

In the New Testament, God's omnipotence is set in the context of the Incarnation; God took on the substance of human flesh

H

and ultimately suffered the most cruel and disgraceful death imaginable at the hands of wicked men, that He might bring man back to Himself, through the conquest of sin and death. The Christian Messiah is a suffering Messiah. Indeed, Jesus Christ suffered and died because He inflexibly obeyed the will of God, with His face set, as a flint, towards death.

From that time onwards, the righteous man was exposed to bitter persecution and, humanly speaking, was a victim of human wickedness. As a result, all followers of Jesus Christ at their baptism take on themselves their "death warrant". And yet in spite of Jesus' suffering and death, God raised Him from the dead and so declared Him the ultimate victor (cf. 2 Cor. 13:4). This victory is a total reversal of all human judgments and of the Old Testament position in particular, Deutero-Isaiah excepted. Since then, the criterion of life changed from individual righteousness to faith in Jesus Christ, and acceptance of the Gospel message. Good works and material prosperity are no longer relevant. Anyone who has tried to live up to the teaching of Jesus Christ knows from his own personal experience, as was the case with St. Paul, that he must always suffer as a direct consequence of his profession of Christianity.

The Incarnation may, however, be yet a ground for another aspect of the omnipotence of God. If one takes seriously the teaching of the Epistle to the Ephesians that God has chosen us (Christians) in Christ from before the foundation of the world that we should be "holy and blameless before Him"; that He has destined us in love to be His sons; and that He has a set purpose determined well beforehand "that the universe, all in heaven and on earth, might be brought into a unity in Christ" (Eph. 1:1-10), we may yet have to ask the question, how far would there have been an Incarnation, apart from sin. Modern theologians, e.g., Westcott and Weston, Mascall and Pittenger, to mention only a few, have already raised this question, in relation to this world which we know and in which Jesus Christ was born, as well as in relation to the universe as it is now understood in the light of modern advances in astronomy.[35]

The present work is too limited in design to allow for a full discussion of the question. But in terms of the African situation, we would say that the Incarnate Christ is the greatest hierophany man has known. He is God manifested in concrete form. The Fourth Gospel, for example, is full of the language of a hierophanic experience. "He that hath seen me hath seen the Father" (14: 9). The miracles Jesus performed are called "signs" by which he "revealed" His glory (2: 11, 6: 14, 12: 18). Jesus is accused of claiming to be on equality with God (5: 18, 10: 33, 19: 7). He claims to be the "apostle of God", and describes Himself as Him whom God did send on a specific mission (5: 23 f., 30; 6: 29, 38 ff.; 7: 16 f., 18, 29; 8: 17 ff., 26; 11: 42; 17: 3, 8, 18 f.). The *I AM* passages of the Gospel are reminiscent of the speech forms appropriate to God in the Old Testament and suggestive of our Lord's claim to divinity.[36] In the Gospel prologue, Jesus is the *Logos* of God who came; and we beheld His glory, "glory as of the only Son from the Father full of grace and truth".

In the African situation, the Supreme God is the father of the deities—implicitly or explicitly: the Yoruba pantheon is roughly estimated at, perhaps, one thousand divinities, and conservatively at 401 gods and goddesses;[37] the Ashanti believe that the Supreme God had various children, of whom *Tano* was the favourite. *Tano*'s descendants are said to be "legion" in number.[38]

On the other hand, for Christians, Jesus Christ is the only Son of God. He is *Monogenes*, i.e., Only-begotten. He is, therefore, the perfect, concrete manifestation of the Power of God. In Him, God became involved in human affairs and in nature. But evil cannot be postulated of Him, although in so far as absolute sovereignty resides in God, moral evil may be said to be perpetrated by His permission. Such permission is, however, purely virtual as both human beings and (we must add) discarnate spirits can act independently of God, resisting His will. All the same, God is "King of them that rule as kings, and Lord of them that rule as lords" (1 Tim. 6: 15), the only Sovereign Ruler of the earth. Christians know that the resurrection of Jesus Christ is the greatest testimony of the omnipotence of God and His sovereignty over nature. Here, then, more than in any other section of Christian thinking, much care and thought has to be exercised to present to African Christians a picture of God which transcends the traditional notions of God in the African environment.

The following lines of approach suggest themselves to us:

(1) African Christians should be helped to cultivate a concept of God which allows for His transcendence and yet removes any suggestions of His indifference to human affairs and experiences. He must be understood, not as a *Deus otiosus*, but as the Creator and Protector of men. Any suggestions that He could not be approached directly but by circuitous routes should be removed by stressing that He is neither a *Deus incertus*, nor a *Deus remotus*, but the God who sent His Son, Jesus Christ, into the world in order to manifest His love for us and to bring us into communion with Himself. The fact of the Incarnation then becomes the ground for introducing the concept of the immanence of God. He identified Himself with man and was intimately involved in the normal human problems of suffering, sickness and death, as well as in the exaltation that comes of human joys and successes. Here we are confronted with a demand for a clear discussion of the problem of "divine passibility", untrammelled by any Greek ideas, and firmly entrenched in the Pauline dictum, "God was in Christ reconciling the world unto Himself" (2 Cor. 5: 19).

(2) Associated with this presentation, we should strive to resolve the serious problem arising from the naïve resignation of many Africans, pagan and Christian alike, to fatalism in times of distress. The pagan attitude to suffering is one of fatalism—the Mende and the Temne, both of Sierra Leone, for example, say, "God had said (decreed) it". One also comes across statements, chiefly from overseas Protestants, to the effect that, for example, a child meets with an accident and dies because God wishes to demonstrate to the parents that He loves him better than they do. Any like comments merely add force to the pagan attitude that such a death is due to some superior hostile external agency. In place of such a fatalistic attitude Christians should seek to cultivate an attitude which accepts that death is an inevitable consequence of birth and it overtakes different individuals differently and at different stages of their life. But, whatever the

circumstances, direct responsibility for a death must not be laid at God's door.

(3) The Christian attitude, firmly anchored in the implications of the Incarnation, should also reject any suggestions that both "good" and "bad" actions, i.e., acts, both socially constructive and morally destructive, can be equally sponsored by God. To the Christian, God is holy and no evil resides in Him. Accordingly those who apprehend that He is holy cultivate a healthy spiritual life. But the Christian understanding of God's holiness is a development of the Hebrew concept which, as has already been pointed out, is associated with the concept of God's glory. For the Christian, therefore, God's holiness is related to His unique all-sovereignty. He is neither fickle nor capricious. At the same time, He is, through Jesus Christ, for ever the Father of all men. As Father, He possesses and demonstrates the omnipotence of love—and so He is long-suffering and forgiving. Jesus Christ is the demonstration of God's attitude to sinful men. He chose us from before the foundation of the world to sonship in Jesus Christ in love ("to be full of love", Eph. 1: 4, N.E.B.). God's love is the criterion of His attitude to creation and to man, and also the stuff of which His own nature consists. Sir John Squire's epigram on the prayers for victory offered by both British and German soldiers during World War I appropriately depicts what could have happened if God was subject to human foibles. The epigram reads:

> God heard the embattled nations sing and shout
> "Gott strafe England!" and "God save the King!"
> God this, God that, and God the other thing.
> "Good God!" said God, "I've got my work cut out!"[39]

God, as Sovereign, however, takes orders from no one. His will prevails always, and in the final analysis Christians pray that the kingdoms of this world shall become the Kingdom of our God and His Christ—and then God shall be all in all. At that point, God's omnipotence shall be supreme and mankind will come to the knowledge that God is love and that that "love will never come to an end" (cf. 1 Cor. 13: 8, N.E.B.).

Chapter 5

A FRESH LITURGICAL APPROACH

SINCE, as we have already noted, the native forms of worship are integral features of the culture of the people, Christian evangelists should seek to redeem the "unholy" features of such worship to the glory of God in Jesus Christ. In this context, one recalls existing successful attempts in Ghana and Nigeria, for example, to adopt African idioms in music for the creation of both songs and tunes. The "shouts" employed in Sierra Leone by various women's Christian groups have been equally successful. The separatist churches already employ rhythmic dances at worship. Further experiments along these lines should therefore be both encouraged and pursued vigorously. But the heart of native African worship is not in its songs and dances *per se*. Song and dance are ingredients of a complex system of liturgical actions—of veneration and adoration; of penitence and forgiveness; of sacrifice and communion—built principally around a host of spirits, ancestral and otherwise.[1]

As was stated earlier, the African, in his desire for concrete manifestations of deity, has postulated the existence of lesser deities and spirits with whom he could make ready contact. These lesser "gods are not invariably good; they have moods, and are sometimes destructive and whimsical. The relationship between the deities and man, and between one deity and another, is conceived in human social terms; the gods speak through their priests; they give promises, they make demands, they issue threats, they show anger as well as pleasure, they listen to prayers, they accept or reject sacrifices, they institute rites in which the worshippers join."[2]

The spirits are thought of in similar terms and so the spirits of the ancestral dead play a prominent part in the social and moral life of the community. The cardinal features of African worship may therefore be discovered by examining (a) ancestor worship, (b) cultic and other rites. It is worth noting that the Supreme God Himself has no votaries, no shrines, no temples and no priests, except perhaps among the Kaffirs, the Kikuyu, the Kposso, the Yoruba, the Akan and the Ewe.[3] But even here, as, for example, among the Akan, the accepted rites are in relation to the lesser deities although Dr. Idowu mentions a cult of *Olodumare* with a priest-chief who performs a daily ritual in *Ile-Ife*.[4] The Kikuyu offer prayers to *Ngai*, but there are no priests dedicated to his worship.

(a) *Ancestor worship.* The participants of ancestor worship are usually "persons related to one another by descent in one line from the same ancestor or ancestors".[5] The rites are, therefore, intended to keep alive the relationship of the living and dead members of this line, and consist of regular sacrifices during which prayers are offered for good crops, fertility, good fortune or success.[6] Sometimes, however, the ancestors are invited to share in the family rejoicing as in the case of the return home of a member of the family after a long absence, or of a wedding. At other times, the rites are purely commemoratory, as on the anniversary of a death, or on festivals celebrating the heroic exploits of the founding fathers. At the rites, the head of the family, or his representative, often the oldest female member of the family, invokes the ancestors by name, one by one, beginning with the latest and ending with the earliest member to die within living memory. But when the clan celebrates, say, a national festival, the order is reversed. In rites invoking the founding fathers, the names are handed down from generation to generation, and so their memories are preserved. Sometimes, the ceremonies are performed at a graveside and at other times at home or at a heroes' shrine. We would add that ancestor worship has a social function, that is, of keeping the clan or tribe together, both living and dead. The main feature of the rites is the offering of sacrifice, which culminates in a communal meal at which it is assumed that the ancestors are present.

The whole complex may be summarized as follows:

(i) *Confession of sin*—it may be of omission, as in cases where the ancestors have not been duly commemorated, or of commission, when there is a feeling that disaster has come because of the misdeeds of the living members.

(ii) *Offering of prayers and sacrifice*—of food and drink; sometimes the food is of the choicest parts of a chicken which has already been killed and its blood allowed to flow into a hole dug in the earth or over the mound of a grave, together with the best portions of other foods which have been prepared. The drink consists of a quantity of water (and spirituous liquor) poured on the ground or over a grave, both to quench the thirst of the ancestors and to refresh them.

(iii) *Omens* are taken by the head of the family or clan, or his representative, to ensure that the offering has been accepted and that the prayers have been heard.

(iv) *The communal meal*. Where there has been an earlier meal, this communal meal consists of what was left of the portions reserved for the offering, previously set apart in a large bowl. In the latter case, there is usually a scramble, everyone present grabbing whatever is at hand. The expression of family *camaraderie* is at its highest at this stage. Everyone is happy, even if one succeeds in grabbing only a tiny portion of the food available.

(b) *Cultic and other rites*. There are various kinds. In West Africa, for example, the cultic rites are performed in cases of illness or ceremonies of the life-cycle, e.g., puberty rites. Even then the ancestors are not completely left out. In the case of illness, the worshippers attribute the disease to their violation of the taboos of their cult. So they start off with a sense of sin and present themselves to the cultic priest for absolution and forgiveness. The constituent elements of this category of rites are:

(i) A full confession of sins committed;

(ii) Omens taken by the priest to ensure that the confession is complete;

(iii) An absolution by the priest; in some cases, this includes the sprinkling of blood—of a chicken or a goat—on the penitents;

(iv) A ritual washing;

(v) A communal meal.

There are also private consultations and prayers which follow the same pattern, although the worshipper, after confessing his sins, merely asks the pardon of the offended spirit or deity by making his offering of sacrifice. In other cases, an oracle is consulted and a cultic priest offers a sacrifice for the person concerned. Confession of guilt is sometimes demanded by force, and then a prescribed sacrifice is offered, which, it is believed, would remove the curse; in most cases a ritual bath is taken, then a meal. The Yoruba *Ebɔ Etutu* is of special interest in this context. The rite is designed to propitiate some evil spirit, and so is performed at night. When it relates to a sick patient, a victim, e.g., a sheep, is killed and the carcase is treated with oil. It is then taken out of the house and may be laid at the foot of an *Iroko* tree (African teak), or left at, say, a cross-roads, as the oracle demands. It is believed that the first person to go past the victim the next morning will attract to himself the *evil* that is being averted from the patient. We would here observe that the use of blood is prominent in most of these rites. Blood is life and is therefore used to establish, preserve, or restore a blood-covenant relationship between all members of the family and, as in the cultic rites, between the deity or spirit and their worshippers.[7]

Is Ancestor Worship, Worship?

To understand some of the basic elements of pagan liturgical action, we must seek to answer the question as to what constitutes worship in the African rites by enquiring into the nature of ancestor worship. Professor Idowu of Ibadan has called attention to the fact that the Yoruba rarely say, "I am going to speak to the 'spirit' of my father; what they say is 'I am going to speak to my father'." He therefore infers that "ancestor worship" is in fact not "worship" but a manifestation of an unbroken family relationship between a deceased parent and his living descendants.[8] This comment is supported by both W. C. Willoughby, who maintains that the discarnate spirits of the ancestors are addressed "in much the same terms" as if they were in the flesh,[9] and by Jomo Kenyatta who prefers the phrase "communion with the ancestors" to "ancestor worship". Jomo Kenyatta observes that "the words 'prayer' and 'worship' ... are reserved for solemn rituals and sacrifices directed to the power of the unseen". So he goes on to say, when "a sheep is sacrificed" to the ancestors "this is a gift"; and what may "seem to an outsider to be prayers directed to the ancestors are nothing but the tributes symbolizing the gifts which the elders would have received had they been alive, and which the living elders now receive". When, therefore, a diviner diagnoses that a family disaster is caused by the anger of the ancestral spirits and a feast is arranged, "the spirits so offended would be invited and offered the feast and asked to communicate with and resume friendly relations with the living family or individuals".[10]

Jomo Kenyatta elsewhere points out the linguistic differences in the phrases for "deity worship", *gothaithaya Ngai*, and "communion with the ancestors", *goitangera ngoma njohi*, respectively, i.e., "to beseech *Ngai* or to worship *Ngai*", and "to pour out or sprinkle beer for the spirits". When on ceremonial occasions both beer and an animal are offered they say, *gothenjera na goitangera ngoma njomi*, i.e., "to slaughter and to pour out beer for the spirits". Here the distinction is quite specific. The Kikuyu "beseech" or "worship" *Ngai*, but they offer gifts to the ancestors. For the private individual this consists of pouring on to the ground for the ancestors a little of whatever one is drinking, and, at the communal level, "a special quantity of beer brewed for presentation to the ancestors" as well as the slaughter of a beast.[11] But *Ngai* "must not be needlessly pestered". A sacrifice is offered to him either on serious occasions like drought or an outbreak of an epidemic or a serious illness,[12] or, on a personal level, at the birth, initiation, marriage and death of a kinsman— when the whole family establish contact with *Ngai* on his behalf.

But, these four crises apart, there seems to be no contact at the level of the individual with *Ngai*. Other crises are referred to the ancestors, e.g., the violation of a taboo,[13] an illness or injury,[14] with the help of a diviner. Monica Wilson also says of Nyakyusa sacrifices, that "the conclusion that this (i.e., the sacrifice) is a communion between the living and the dead is inescapable".[15] They worship the now deified hero ancestors also designated as creators, but the dominant theme in their rituals, and more so in the rituals celebrated by private persons, is their kinship ties.[16]

At a typical sacrificial rite they pray:

"May the children sleep, may we all sleep, may it rain,
may there be much food, may milk be plentiful."

"Then follows a communion in which young 'grandchildren' of the dead share of the sacred meat and beer. The shades eat together, ..."[17]

Another prayer reads, *inter alia*: "We pray to *Kyala*.
May theft go away. Give us food and beans and millet,
may we eat and be satisfied ..."[18]

One factor which seems to determine Nyakyusa worship is the "anger" of the ancestors. For the Nyakyusa, "harmony" is a *desideratum*; and this holds true both in relation to the living members with kinship ties, or with the living *vis-à-vis* the dead.[19] Dr. Idowu also refers to hero-worship, presumably in respect of the Yoruba pantheon to which prominent figures like *Oduduwa* and *Sango* have been added.[20] By widening the scope of the community of the ancestors, Dr. Idowu seems to allow for a worship of (at least) some of the ancestors—the deified—as well as the element of communion which perhaps may be postulated for most.

Ulli Beier, on the other hand, specifically asserts that the Yoruba "worship their ancestors", and adds that the "pagan" Yoruba attributes misfortune to an angered ancestor. In cases which cannot be easily resolved the contestants will go to the tomb of an ancestor, offer prayer and sacrifices. "Then they will evoke his spirit and take an oath. 'May the one who has not spoken the truth in this matter die within seven days'—or some such formula. The Yoruba will remember his ancestors at every meal, and he will never fail to pour a libation to them."[21] Writers on the Akan of Ghana in West Africa, either explicitly use the phrase "worship of the ancestors" (so Busia),[22] or talk of the propitiation of the ancestral spirits (so Rattray, Meyerowitz).[23] In any case, offerings are made to them; they are propitiated; their aid is invoked in times of crises and on festivals like the *Adae* and the *Adwera*. Rattray observes that "the predominant influences in the Ashanti religion are neither 'Saturday Sky-god' nor 'Thursday Earth-goddess', nor even the hundreds of gods (*abosom*), with which it is true the land is filled, but are the *samanfo*, the spirits of the departed forbears of the clan".[24] So indeed "before partaking of wine or spirits", "the Ashanti pours a little on the ground from the cup . . . for the shades of his ancestors".[25]

Busia has recorded some details of an *Adwera* Festival at Wenchi, in Ghana, which may be useful in this discussion. On the first night, Tuesday, the women sang "songs of thanksgiving" to the gods, the Supreme Being and to the ancestors, "for the gift of a good harvest, for life and children, or offered prayers for the same things". On the following day, Wednesday, the chief spokesman of the district (*Ɔkyeame*) poured libations of rum and offered, as sacrifice, a sheep provided by the chief. At the libations, he mentioned each of the reigning chief's predecessors by name, saying,

> "'Here is drink' (*as he poured the libations*) or 'here is meat' (*as he offered the meat*). All of you, grandsires, by your help the year has come round again; your grandson (the chief) has come this morning to bring you a sheep and drink; grant him health, prosperity to the Wenchi people; let the celebrations about to begin pass peacefully. Blessing, blessing."

On the Monday of the second week, the central rite was performed. A procession, consisting of women carrying food in brass pans, a row of boys carrying palm-wine and locally brewed beer from maize corn, the chief's own mother, the queen-mother and other senior women of the royal families in the town, marched to a sacred tree. Two bearers brought water from a nearby stream. Seated beneath the tree, the chief's mother offered the food and the drink, mentioning each departed chief and then each queen-mother by name and saying,

> "Here is food (or drink, *as is appropriate*); all of you receive this and eat (or drink); the year has come round again; today we celebrate it; bring us blessing; blessing to the chief who sits on your stool; health to the people; let women bear children; let the men prosper in their undertakings; life to all; we thank you for the good harvest, for standing behind us. Blessing, blessing, blessing."

The attendant crowd reply: "Blessing, blessing, blessing."[26]

This type of prayer is typical of those offered by the Yoruba, which Dr. Idowu describes as having an "objective petitionary character".[27]

In Sierra Leone, one comes across similar prayers to the dead among the Creole, the Temne and the Mende, for example. The occasions range from individual to national crises—happy occasions like marriage (among the Creole), or initiation ceremonies at the end of *Poro* among the Mende, or commemorations of a death.

The general impression gained from a study of the prayers offered to the ancestors is that they do not differ intrinsically from the prayers offered by the Kikuyu to *Ngai*. Even Jomo Kenyatta admits that the Kikuyu "expect *Mwene-Nyaga* to answer their prayers favourably in return for the present given", i.e., the animal sacrifice. This law of "give and take" governs the prayers to the ancestors which we have cited above. Again, he states that when a person falls ill and is directed by a diviner to communicate with the spirit of an offended ancestor who is thought to have caused the illness, "Atonement is made and the invalid recovers".[28] Of course, when this treatment fails, an approach is made to *Ngai*, jointly by the ancestors and the living members of the family concerned. Jomo Kenyatta also mentions one other instance of appeal by the body of living and dead members of a family. This is in respect of a person who has been struck by lightning. What is significant here is that such a victim is generally thought to have been daring to look upwards (during a thunder-storm) "to see *Mwene-Nyaga* stretching himself and cracking his joints in readiness for his active service to chase away or smash his enemies".[29] We can see no difference between propitiating a god, and making atonement with an ancestor, as far as intention goes. One common factor can be isolated from all the other aspects of the two rites: that is, anger, referred to as the anger of the ancestor,[30] on the one hand, and the wrath of *Ngai* on the other. The first is described as calling for atonement, the second for propitiation, both producing the same effect—the restoration of good relations between the parties, i.e., communication.

We would, therefore, suggest that although Jomo Kenyatta has drawn a distinction between the two actions, yet he has only produced a distinction without a difference. The law of "give and take" which determines Kikuyu worship of *Ngai* also operates in the prayers to the ancestors cited above from West Africa, and operates in the language implied in the so-called Kikuyu "communion with the ancestors".[31] The attitude of the Neuer in this regard is interesting. According to Evans-Pritchard, they seem to direct their prayers to God although they recognize certain spirits of the air and of the earth, as well as spirits of their ancestors. These are distinct spirits, but, being spirit, they are all children of God or refractions of His hypostasis.[32] So, whilst it can be said that prayers are offered to the spirits, it is also held that these prayers are offered to God. At the same time, samples of these prayers show the same structure as those cited earlier, e.g.,

"Our father, it is thy universe, it is thy will, let us be at peace, let the souls of the people be cool, thou art our father, remove all evil from our path."[33]

As Evans-Pritchard himself rightly observes, "They are asking God for deliverance from evil, so that they may have peace, denoted by a variety of images with emotional and ideational relatedness—sleep, lightness, ease, coolness, softness, prayer, the domestic hearth, abundant life, and life as it should be according to the nature of the person".[34] We would therefore maintain that Africans do offer prayers to their ancestors and, for the purpose of this work, such prayers constitute a form of worship. Even Dr. Idowu says, without any qualification, that to the Yoruba, "Egungun designates the spirit of the deceased to which *worship* [italics, mine] is offered at the ancestral shrine".[35]

Next to ancestor worship are the forms of worship related to nature deities, cultic and non-cultic. These follow set rules and must be correctly performed to be effective. Dr. Idowu tells us that "in Yoruba (cultic) worship, there is nothing of the nonconformists' go-as-you-please style"—this is a Methodist minister speaking![36] The devotees must all be ceremonially clean. This may mean the avoidance of sexual intercourse immediately before worship or making sure of a "thorough washing" afterwards, or worst of all, having an "impure heart". The worship, private or public, consists of a salutation to the god and an acknowledgement of his providential care; the worshippers pour a libation of water and make their petitions. The attitude of the god to his devotees and their future prospects is determined by divining with kola-nuts; where a priest is in attendance he blesses the participants. The petitions made are for "material blessings", like protection from sickness and death, gifts of longevity, children, prosperity in enterprises, protection of relatives near and distant; blessings on all well-wishers and damnation on all ill-wishers.[37]

At this point it may be useful to draw attention to the misconception that the Yoruba phrase for "prayer" is *she orisha*, literally, "to make the god", and the consequential inferences drawn from it.[38] Dr. Idowu does not use the phrase, although he tells us that one may "create" an *Egungun*, a masked figure assumed to represent the visit on earth of a deceased ancestor.[39] According to Ulli Beier, when the Ifa oracle orders a man "to worship his ancestor" he then arranges for a mask to be made, takes it, with "appropriate presents", to the head of the *Egungun* cult (the *Alagba*) who secretly appoints a member of the *Egungun* society to wear it.[40] In this context the *Egungun* is actually made, its wearer being expected to impersonate the ancestor. But the phrase *she orisha* may also mean "do the god". The verb *she*, which means "do", seems to have specialized cultic use, and therefore comes to mean "dramatize the god". The essence of this phrase therefore seems to imply the element of possession. Ulli Beier says that "at the height of the dance every true *Egungun* will enter into a state of possession, when he will speak in a new voice." Robin Horton says of a Kalabari masker—a human actor who dramatizes the presence of one of the personalized gods of the community—"though in cold blood he acknowledges the distinction between himself and the god of the mask, it is his every movement that compels the presence of the god with him in the dancing arena". He then adds, "It is not hard for elation to blur the boundary of his identity a little, and not far to go before his everyday consciousness gives place altogether to something quite alien to it".[41] This is the real import of the phrase *she orisha*. The Yoruba say the phrase, as it stands, is elliptical. The complete statement is *she orisha Ogun* or *Shango*, etc.; i.e., "celebrate (as is due) the festival of the (relevant) god". This comment fits in with Idowu's "creating" the *Egungun*. The Yoruba verb to "pray" in cultic worship is Ɛbɛ, which seems to be cognate with Ɛbɔ "sacrifice".[42] It must be noted that the Yoruba stress as far as possible "a harmony between the personality of the medium and that of the god"[43] as an ideal. J. V. Taylor and Jahnheinz Jahn have obviously read more into the phrase than the ordinary Yoruba understand it to mean.

We may therefore summarize this discussion so far by saying that Africans do worship their ancestors and divinities. This worship consists of prayers, sacrifices, and divination on communal occasions, or prayers and divinations on private occasions. For the latter a priest may or may not be present, although it would be correct to think of the owner of a personal deity as its private priest. All such forms of worship are built around certain ritual acts, which themselves demand certain preliminary requirements of priest and worshippers, for example, a "pure

heart" towards one's kinsmen as among the Neuer, or an inter-
mission of the sex-act before the day of the performance as
among the Ga and the Akan. The prayers themselves consist of
petitions related to the welfare of the worshippers, their children,
their harvests, peace and goodwill in the country. We would
repeat that, although prayers are offered to the Supreme God by
a few groups—the Ashanti, the Neuer and the Kaffirs, for
instance—African tribal worship is directed for the most part to
the ancestors or the divinities.

SOME BASIC FEATURES OF CHRISTIAN WORSHIP

In spite of everything we have said on ancestor worship, it
falls far short of Christian worship. To us Christians, worship
demands the surrender of the self to God. This embraces adoration and thanksgiving; confession and declaration of forgiveness; petition and intercession; the reading and preaching of the
Word of God in varying combinations and with slightly differing
emphases to suit the occasion. But, in every case, there is a
realization of the Presence of God which produces a feeling of
nothingness. The totally abandoned worshipper also experiences
a unique sense of release leading to exhilaration. These two notes
represent what Dr. Lowther Clarke describes as two moments
of Christian worship—the one positive and the other negative.
At the negative moment, "Our words quiver into silence; our
thoughts lose themselves in infinity; our feelings tremble before
the formless; our righteousness becomes uncleanness. Before the
greatness of God we are nothing." At the positive moment,
"Our human means of approach are given back to us transformed; Christ, True Man by virtue of His Incarnation, perfects
and presents to the Father our poor, imperfect worship. Our
words, our prayers, our actions are accepted 'in the Beloved'.
But they are given back to us consecrated and enlarged. Our
thoughts still have the quality of mystery behind and beyond
them; we can praise God with the understanding ... but we
know that the theme is too high for us. We repeat over to ourselves the 'evidences' of His Love and Goodness but we know

I

that they far transcend 'our benumbed conceiving'; we express our emotion at His Beauty and Greatness, but we know that we only hear a whisper of His Ways."

Dr. Clarke goes on to say "True Christian Worship, then, is neither a formless ecstasy nor a dry 'parade-service', but a consecration of all our faculties to His Glory". In a footnote, he adds the rider, "We use the word (Worship) in the more special sense of those parts of the service (e.g., the Sanctus) where the human side seems to fade away, where definite petition and thanksgiving are hushed, and we praise God for what He is".[44] Dr. Clarke has put his finger on the vital factor of Christian worship. It is essentially the adoration of God as Sovereign Lord of the world, Creator, Redeemer, Provider and Sustainer of man and nature. Frail man therefore must wait for Him in silence, completely abandoned to His will.[45]

TOWARDS THE TRANSFIGURATION OF AFRICAN WORSHIP FOR CHRIST

We must now raise the inevitable question as to how the transferable features previously described as present in ancestor and cultic worship may be transformed and brought within the orbit of the Christian faith. This is a question of the highest significance, with many sides to it. We propose, however, to limit our discussion to the following factors:

(1) THE TRANSFORMATION OF THE AFRICAN CONCEPT OF GOD

Africans should be helped to cultivate a new conception of God, as the God who though transcendent has become immanent in Jesus Christ, whom Christians know as "the image of the invisible God" (Col. 1 : 15, cf. Heb. 1 : 3), and through whom they address their worship to God. It is worth recalling that Mr. Nketia of Ghana has suggested that the Africanization of Christian worship should be planned around the worship of Christ "as the risen Lord", at the same time taking into consideration "the Reformation principle of bringing home 'to the minds' and understanding of ordinary people" the great truths of the Christian faith through "the translation of the Bible, the growth of liturgies in local languages and the creation, adoption and use of hymns in local languages".[46] He further stresses that Christian worship should be so determined "that the African worshipper can understand and feel deeply as he worships"[47] and that "even if the same techniques of prayer were adopted—kneeling, standing, prostrating—the Christian prayer may be vastly different from the non-Christian prayer".[48] These are important criteria, with which we would concur. But we would point out that African culture is not static. In the old days Africans used to attribute freaks of nature or any extraordinary qualities of their fellow-men to witchcraft,[49] jinns and other supernatural agencies, including the ancestral dead. A huge mountain, a shady dell, a large-spreading cotton tree, a huge outcrop of rock or of rock-formations like the Olumɔ Rock in Abeokuta, Nigeria, all once created the sense of the numinous. But today the bulldozer and the tractor, the aeroplane and the wireless, have increasingly led to a change of emphasis.

The old beliefs still persist, but the bulldozer has also been seen pulling up from the roots the trees which once constituted a sacred grove, and, interesting to relate, with no adverse effects on the operatives or on the towns. On the contrary, roads have been built and townships improved as a result. Indeed, the aeroplane and the wireless have become the examples, *par excellence*, of the efficiency of the "witchcraft" of western peoples. A transference, conscious or unconscious, of values has accordingly taken place. The numinous elements in the life of the primitive African uninfluenced by western culture have now been displaced by a sense of wonder aroused by mechanical power. Equally, the growth of industrialism and the exodus from the villages to the towns have led to a relaxation of the moral sanctions inherent in tribal life. Urbanization has led to serious moral lapses. But worse still is the increasing influence of secularist thinking, produced perhaps chiefly by the increasing study of the natural sciences in the secondary schools and the new university institutions which are springing up all over the

African continent.[50] Young Africans are being exposed to categories of thought which are contrary to their native background of spirits and witchcraft.

Cognate with this regard for progress is the associated belief in an evolutionary development of the universe and the world. God is no longer the Creator of the universe; indeed, it has become a source of personal pride to many to accept the view that the universe has evolved out of gaseous nebulae, with an emphasis on the word "evolved". God is now an obtrusion.[51] These new initiates into scientific modes of thought tend to lapse easily into a materialist philosophy of life. And yet, in spite of this tremendous change in outlook, many well-educated Africans, some of them Christians, turn to native traditional beliefs in times of distress. It is therefore difficult to disagree with Dr. Busia that Christianity is still "alien" to the African.[52] If we could transform the content of the indigenous African belief in God and therefore teach Africans to worship Him, we might be able to Africanize Christianity, whilst keeping it within the circle of world Christianity.

(2) THE TRANSFORMATION OF THE AFRICAN'S ATTITUDE TO THE SPIRITS

In view of the widespread practice of both ancestor and cultic worship, our African brethren should be helped to cultivate a new attitude to the spirits, in the hope of determining a basic form both applicable and acceptable to Christianity. In particular, we should strive to eliminate the worship both of the ancestral and cultic spirits. We would here repeat that the worship of cultic spirits, though more extensive, is not essentially distinct from ancestor worship, because the ancestors are generally associated with the spirits of the cults. According to Dr. C. G. Baeta a discussion of "prayers to ancestors" might readily provide "all the material for a theological battle-royal . . .".[53] Is such a battle-royal inevitable? Mr. Nketia's comments mentioned earlier dispose of such a suggestion. Indeed, Dr. Baeta himself, after referring to the letter of Pope Gregory to Mellitus, A.D.

601, made the important comment, "apparently the Great Pope Gregory himself . . . believed that the same sacrifices as were previously offered to idols, could later fitly be offered to God, because they were then no longer the same sacrifices".[54] This last statement does seem to us to be a good talking point for the Christianization of African cultic worship by the Church. But let us first enunciate a few principles to guide our "talking", viz.:

(1) That "the Church is not a cultic group concerned with holding services but a body of people charged with a mission".[55] J. G. Davies, who makes this statement, does not define the mission to which he refers. But we would say, in the language of Ephesians 3: 10, that the mission of the Church is to make known "to principalities and powers in the heavenly places the multiform wisdom of God". Such a definition could in our opinion cut across the clan and tribal limitations inherent in cultic rites and establish the all-Sovereignty of God.

(2) That belief in the spirits, however real it may be to those who hold it, is not based on any personal relationship. Indeed, apart from the ancestral spirits, none of the objects of pagan worship has any historical origin. To the Christian, on the other hand, Jesus Christ is both an historical Person, an elder Brother and a personal Friend who came to the world to manifest the love of God for mankind (John 3: 16; Romans 8: 28). This fact of the friendship of Jesus, who is also our elder Brother, is of vital importance in helping Africans to appreciate God's attitude to the world and to the sufferings of mankind. Through the Incarnation of Jesus, God has Himself come to understand the pains and agony of human suffering and therefore always stands in with human beings in their distress (cf. 2 Cor. 1: 3–10).

So real can the experience of God's Presence be in times of acute distress that St. Paul could hear the message:

"My grace is sufficient for you, for my power is made perfect in weakness" (2 Cor. 12: 9, R.S.V.).

He himself could say,

"I will all the more gladly boast of my weaknesses, that the power of Christ may rest upon me" (*ibidem*).

Amulets and pagan sacrificial rites, on the other hand, offer no such assurance. They evoke no voluntary self-surrender in those who trust in them.

(3) That sacrifice is both acceptable to God and is man's duty to Him (Romans 12: 1). For the Christian, this fact is evident from the life and death of Jesus Christ, an event described in the language of the Book of Common Prayer as "a full, perfect and sufficient Sacrifice, oblation and satisfaction for the sins of the whole world"[56] (cf. 1 Cor. 5: 7; Hebrews *passim*). Sacrifice may therefore be offered by Christian worshippers and should be offered provided it is by way of the Sacrifice of Christ, in self-offering at the Eucharist when the worshippers can identify themselves with the self-offering of Jesus Christ.[57]

(4) That the sacrifice of Christ betokens the establishment of a blood-covenant-relation between God and man, i.e., the New Covenant of the New Testament. This covenant, though akin to the Old Covenants with the Jews, is of a superior *genus*. In particular, it is associated with a new creation; its members live in a relation of sonship to God as Father, through the mediation of His Son Jesus Christ (Rom. 8: 29; Col. 3: 9 f.).

Let us now return to the sacrifices and prayers offered to the ancestral dead in African worship to see how the "unholy" can be transformed into the "holy". To get a proper perspective, let us first look back briefly at traditional Christian practice. In the early centuries of Christianity, "There were cemetery chapels, situated in burying-places and used for funeral services and masses, and for anniversaries and other commemorations, as well as for the funeral *agape*. . . . It often happened that the cemetery chapel was built near or even over the tomb of a martyr." The writer then adds that "The faithful loved to hold meetings, either liturgical or otherwise, on the sites where the heroes of the faith reposed".[58] In particular, "the anniversary of the martyrdom of St. Polycarp (A.D. 155) was instituted at Smyrna immediately after his death".[59] In the Malkite Horologion, there are several invocations of St. Mary and various other saints requesting them to "supplicate" the Lord for the worshippers. One comprehensive invocation reads as follows:

"Our Lady, Mary, Mother of God, intercede for us sinners. All the holy angels and heavenly archangels, intercede for us sinners. Holy Mar John, forerunner of Christ and baptist, intercede for us sinners. Our Lords the Prophets, Moses and Aaron, Elijah and Elisha, and all the Prophets who wrought miracles, intercede for us sinners. Saints, Apostles, and the worshipful Mar Peter and Paul, and all the Apostles, intercede for us sinners; the holy Martyrs, Mar George, Mar Theodorius, Mar Cosmas, and Damiarus, Mar Sergius and Bacchus, Mar Demetrius and Barkobius, Mar Mercurius, and Mar Menas the Martyr, Mar Kyriakus and Julitta, his mother, and Mar Samone and her seven children; and all the saints who fought for Christ's sake, intercede for us sinners. Our holy fathers, Basilius, and Gregorius and John, the golden-tongued, and the wonderful Nicolaus, and all saints, intercede for us sinners. Our righteous fathers, Mar Simeon and Mar Saba, Euthymius, Gerasimus, Charito, Theodosius, Antonius, Pachomius, Ephramius, Onuphrius, and all our righteous fathers who dwell in the desert, intercede on our behalf, sinners, by the incomprehensible power of the precious, saving cross."[60]

It would therefore be difficult to deny a similarity of "form" between the practice already hallowed by Christian tradition and pagan ancestral worship. The veneration and commemoration of saints have always been part of the life of the Catholic tradition of the Church. Modern trends in the Reformed Churches show increasing sympathy with the practice, such as we find for example in the writings of a leading theologian of the Reformed Church of France, Max Thurian. In discussing Mariology, he says, "Christ cannot ever be separated from the Church and from His witnesses, and a Protestant piety which rejects all veneration of Christ in the Church, its hierarchy, and its saints falls into an individualist spirituality, wherein Christ is sought solely and directly in the heart of the Trinity without the assembly and communion of the Church and of the saints".[61] We might here say that Max Thurian is expressing the New Testament language of Hebrews 12: 22–24 which he himself later quotes:

"You have come to Mount Sion, the city of the living God, the heavenly Jerusalem, to myriads of angels in festal gathering, to the assembly of the first-born registered in heaven, to the God of all as judge, to the spirits of just men made perfect, to Jesus who mediates the new covenant, and to the sprinkled blood whose message is nobler than Abel's" (Moffatt's translation).

Referring to the role of Mary in the Church, Max Thurian goes on to say, "the role that Mary ought to play, like the apostles and all the saints, must also be manifested in piety and in liturgy. A Church which despises the communion of saints, of all the saints, present and past, here and elsewhere, risks losing itself in individualism and sectarianism."[62] He therefore defends "the commemoration of the saints in the Church" as "a form of perfect love. . . . They all guide us and sustain us in each day's combat; in loving them we love Christ in them, whose perfect image they for their part reflect. 'Be ye imitators of me, even as I also am of Christ', St. Paul says to us (I Cor. 11: 1)."[63]

Later on, the same writer enquires "whether any request for the intercession of the saints must necessarily be considered as foreign to the strict evangelical spirit". Again, he asks, "Are not prayers for one another, intercession and the request for intercession, the most significant manifestations of the mystery of the communion of saints in the Church?"[64] His answer is most instructive, viz., that "Intercession is, with the Word and Eucharist, the most firm cement of the Christian community. The wider the field of intercession, the more the Church grows to the dimensions of the Body of Christ. . . . If we can ask the intercession of a living brother, why, in the certitude that we have of the life in Christ of those who have left their bodies, may we not ask dead saints to pray, when we ourselves are drawing nigh to the city of the living God and to innumerable hosts of angels and to the general assembly and Church of the firstborn? Will not this strengthen our faith in eternal life?" Later, he adds, ". . . intercession strengthens the sense of the *koinonia*". Max Thurian does not approve of "prayers for the dead". At the same time, he clearly appreciates the value of invoking the intercession of "those who live close" to Christ.[65] Max Thurian's last comment is reminiscent of the attitude of the Yoruba or the Kikuyu or the Nyakyusa. But he is using a Christian plank as a spring-board.[66]

(3) THE TRANSFORMATION OF THE RATIONALE OF THE AFRICAN'S SENSE OF WORSHIP

Looking back on what has been said so far about the African situation, we may isolate three facets of cultic worship. First, the worshippers are suppliants who seek to win the favour of their deity. Adoration may be part of this process but their chief act is petitionary. Second, the offer of sacrifice provides a medium of communication between the petitioners and the deity. Third, a priest representing the deity offers absolution and healing to the worshippers after presenting their sacrifice to the deity. His work follows a rigid rule of set forms and formularies which he carefully learns beforehand and to which he must always adhere in an inflexible manner. The priest can, therefore, be said to fulfil a three-fold role:

(a) He is the person to whom people who are living under abnormal circumstances resort and from whom they seek to gain relief. The element of abnormality is the real criterion here. One feels a headache or one's baby has a fever. First reactions always are to find a herbal curative. Invariably some such curative is used for several days and if the patient reacts favourably to the treatment no further steps are taken. But, when the patient does not respond to such treatment, he himself or his parents and relatives begin to grow anxious and the illness is attributed to other than natural causes. They then consult a diviner for his professional advice. The latter then diagnoses the cause of the illness and directs the patient or his representatives to a cultic priest for the cure. In other words, the patient goes to the diviner for guidance and to the priest, to whom he is guided, for healing.[67] Abnormality is also attributed to the major crises of life, especially to initiation. The young person who has grown to the age of puberty, and is to be initiated into one or other of the adult tribal societies of the area, is regarded as undertaking a step important enough to be out of all proportion to his previous mode of life. In some cases, the rites specifically include cultic worship. In others, the cultic priest is invited to perform preliminary ceremonies which would ensure the success of the rites. Such ceremonies naturally imply the offering of sacrifices to the ancestors and to the "god" of the cult. The *raison d'être* of such ceremonies includes invoking the support and protection of the cultic god as well as of the ancestral spirits—principally those of earlier officiants. The officiants of the cult thus feel confident to undertake the initiation rites with sanguine hopes of success, and parents of the initiates become equally confident of their safety during the rites. The community as a whole also register their full support of the rites and the session is started in a confident and happy mood by all, save, perhaps, the initiates who are usually apprehensive of what lies ahead of them.

(b) Since sin and sickness are closely related in tribal religious thought, the cultic priest provides the community with the appropriate psychiatric treatment through a clinic built around a cultic spirit. Where the wholeness of the society is disturbed by an offence, the priest first performs certain expiatory rites, and, in some cases, exacts a punishment, e.g., a fine or flagellation for incest, and then restores the offender(s) to the community. The patient(s) are known to leave the cultic shrine either feeling well, or confident of early recovery. These rites are usually performed in public. In other cases, as, for example, lack of success, the priest performs, either privately or in the presence of close relatives, a purificatory rite, designed to remove the trouble, and the suppliants again return home confident of success.

(c) The cultic priest is the only person in his community who has direct access to the cultic spirit. He alone can enter the sacred shrine where one exists. Only he can handle the emblems of the cult and the sacred vessels, without fear of bringing down harm upon himself. He is thus the spokesman of the cultic spirit and so he alone can reveal his will to the supplicating worshippers. He is therefore endowed with sacrosanctity. He is a sacred person who is highly revered and often feared in his community. He is expected to lead a highly moral life, with special reference to his sex activities. As a result, in some cases, only an old man past sex activities may be a priest. Where sex is not taboo he must exercise it with due care, especially at the times when he performs as a priest. Margaret Field says that, among the Ga of Ghana, a man who had married one or several wives before assuming the duties of a priest was required to divorce them and marry a young wife "carefully chosen for her worth from among certain priestly families".[68] A high standard of moral integrity was therefore required of the wife also. The priest must also be trustworthy. The full and frank confessions he demands of suppliants must never be repeated to others. A suppliant can therefore confidently speak the truth in order to ensure complete relief from his troubles. Equally, the cultic priest, as the mouthpiece of the "god", absolves the penitents in the name of his "god", and prescribes forms of behaviour consonant with the will of the "god".

The cultic priest thus has a dual function as the intermediary between his "god" and man; he is, at once, both the agent through whom society preserves its wholeness—jointly and severally—among its members, and also the medium through whom the will of the cultic spirit is revealed to man. So he can dispense the forgiveness granted by his "god". Since, however, all the cults are associated with, at least, some of the ancestral spirits, this forgiveness assumes an extended character and provides a means of restoring the penitent sinner back to the normal human relationships approved by society.

We are now in a position to examine the ways in which Christian thought and practice may be employed in the African situation.

Here we shall limit our consideration to the central act of Christian worship, viz., the Eucharist. This rite embraces various elements of which we shall mention only a few:

(i) The gathering of the worshippers for adoration, confession, thanksgiving, petition and intercession.
(ii) The offering of a sacrifice of the worshippers in union with the sacrifice of Christ on Calvary.
(iii) The recalling of Jesus by the celebration of the Eucharist.
(iv) The identification of the worshippers, already united into Christ's death and resurrection at baptism, with the Body of Christ; this factor embraces the fact of the membership of Christians in the New Age inaugurated by Christ's resurrection.

Of course, the central factor is the sacrifice of Christ and the sacrifice of His Body the Church, offered as a propitiation for our sins. If we accept the Johannine tradition supported by the writer of the Epistle to the Hebrews that Jesus Christ was both Priest and Victim, we may also postulate that, as in every other case, the Church now re-enacting the sacrifice of Christ must do so by means of a priesthood.

The essential interpretation of Christ's ministry is that, by His death, He became the mediator between God and man (2 Cor. 5: 19) and between Jew and Gentile (Eph. 2: 13 f.). This, His priestly act, is continued in heaven as a sacrifice slain (ἐσφάγμενον) for us. Indeed the phrase, εἰς ἀνάμνησιν, has been said to be sacrificial, although the actual usage of the noun in such a context seems to be rare.[69] Gregory Dix, however, interprets the word "anamnesis" and its cognate verb as implying a "'recalling' or 're-presenting' before God an event in the past, so that it becomes *here and now operative by its effects*". He then observes that the New Testament and the second century writers interpret the anamnesis of the Eucharist as a "re-calling" or "re-presenting" before God the sacrifice of Christ, thus making it here and now operative by its effects on the communicants.[70] Accordingly, he later asserts that "what the Body and Blood of Christ were on Calvary and *before and after*—'an

offering and a sacrifice to God for us'—that they are now in the
Eucharist, the anamnesis not of His death only but 'of Me'—of
the Redeemer in the fulness of His offered Self, and work and
life and death, perpetually accepted by the Father in the World
to come".[71] Anamnesis thus is a doing—a sacrifice—"the
perpetual 'recalling' and energizing in the Church of that one
sacrifice".[72] This is a priestly act, performed by the Church in
response to our Lord's command.[73] Here then is a continuous
series of actions based on the once-for-all act of Jesus in *illo
tempore*, when He suffered under Pontius Pilate, was crucified,
was dead and buried, but God raised Him from the dead. At the
same time, we believe that Jesus continues His earthly work in
heaven where, in His eternal priesthood, He sustains the sacrifice
He had offered by always pleading on our behalf (cf. Heb. 7: 25).
Africans understand this idiom, though on a lower plane. The
Kwotto of Nigeria appeal, in times of drought, to their "deceased
chiefs, the High Priests of Ancestor Worship in the Spirit
World, . . . to give the living rain".[74]

The Kikuyu solicit the co-operation of their ancestral spirits
in offering prayers jointly to *Mwene-Nyaga* on behalf of one
who has been struck by lightning as this is, in effect, punishment
for a form of blasphemy.[75] The Mende of Sierra Leone have a
phrase which means "tell-taste" or (?) test, i.e., to indicate one's
intention of seeking advice by way of consultation with, and
appeal to, one's superiors. This phrase has a strong law-court-
room flavour. A decision is arrived at by the court and one or
both of the contestants then says, "Let me consult my family"—
wiser heads, perhaps. He may also use the phrase in regard to an
appeal to his ancestral spirits, and sometimes, though not usually,
to God, in cases where all hope of redress for a wrong fails. The
appeal to the ancestral spirits implies that, being spirit, they can
more readily seek the counsel of God who is Himself Spirit.
They are thus playing the role of priests.

In the light of the preceding arguments, we see no difficulty
in presenting Jesus Christ to African converts as the eternal High
Priest to whom we can resort in times of anxiety, depression and
worry. If Jesus is the High Priest, then we could go on to say

that our anamnesis of Him "is the appropriation of his death and endless life, and all the benefits thereof".[76] This notion also embraces the further notion that the Church is the Body of Christ. The means of appropriating the death of Christ is to enter mystically into that death and therefore the offering by the Church of herself to God. This is a sacrificial act (cf. John 17: 19). Such an act can best be performed by one who is not merely accepted as a minister, but who specifically takes on the office and function of a priest, viz.: to mediate, offer sacrifice, absolve and bless. He mediates between God and His people, offers sacrifice to God on behalf of the people, absolves them of their sins, after due confession has been made, and blesses them, in the Name of God. Such peripheral requirements as eschewing sex-relations prior to performing the duties of the priestly office are not in fact incompatible with Christian practice. In the *Priest's Book of Private Devotion,** there exists an interesting rubric which reads:

> "The priest who is about to celebrate must be in a state of grace and fasting from midnight ..."[77]

Other prayers in the same book stress purity; but one specifically devoted to chastity includes the statement:

> "Suffer me at no time to pollute my body, which is the temple of the Holy Ghost, with any uncleanness ..."[78]

We would suggest that, for a ministry in which celibacy is not the accepted norm of life, the "state of grace" and the "uncleanness" referred to in the excerpts given above may be rightfully interpreted as relating to sex relations. The African cults, as well as the spiritual Churches, stress the need for avoiding sex relations immediately before the performance of priestly acts. Can orthodox Christians claim to hold dissimilar views on the subject?

We must now enquire into the *raison d'être* of the sacrifices offered both to the ancestors and the cultic spirits. Are they really bribes offered to "flatter a god and so buy his favour"?[79]

* Of Anglican derivation.

Again, how accurate is Westermann's estimate, for example, that "a basic factor in pagan religion is that it tries to make the divine powers an instrument of man's personal welfare"?[80] Much of the evidence relating to the supernatural leads us to conclude that the god or ancestor who is worshipped and the totem that is first venerated and later worshipped are assumed to have blood kinship with the family, clan, tribe or nation. We recall that when a sacrifice is offered to a cultic god or the ancestors, the offerer identifies himself with the victim or the gift offered, usually by laying his hands on it, thereby declaring the victim his representative. This identification indicates that the offerer has consecrated himself, through the victim, to the honour of the god. The offerer then prepares himself in the expiatory as well as the propitiatory rites for the purification by confession. He thus acknowledges the sovereignty of the cultic spirit and submits himself to its will. The rites also provide an opportunity to remove all forms of bitterness and to restore happy relationships (a cool heart) among kinsmen. Whenever there is a meal, the food is generally shared by a group of people.

Individuals are usually accompanied by their relatives or friends when they go to offer a sacrifice. The god, spirit or spirits are also believed to partake of the meal. In special cases, the god or totemic spirit is itself assumed to be the food which the devotees share. Yerkes has observed that the common meal has always been "an agent in maintaining the unity of the group"; it provided for primitive man the source of power other than his own. The tendency to ceremonialism thus introduced by sharing a common meal became a necessity at times when "human finiteness was more acute, as before going on a trek or striking camp, or before entering a battle, or after the successful performance of these acts, or after failure, that they who had failed might lay greater hold on the Power".[81] Soon the "Power" sought became personified in a god or spirit who was later venerated and to whom allegiance was paid.

This interpretation of the *rationale* of sacrificial rites is supported by H. J. Rose who, in a discussion of *Numen* and *Mana*, suggests that the purpose of sacrifice is to "increase" in power the god to whom the offering is made, "presumably by receiving the life of the victim, certainly by being fed on such holy food as its duly consecrated flesh, or the cereal offerings, also duly consecrated, which may replace or accompany it".[82] Elsewhere, in association with O. Skutch, he says that "to increase the power of a deity by appropriate ritual seems to be the aim and object of ancient sacrifice in its earliest forms before it was thought of as a present to win his favour; ..."[83] We would go on to say that acts cognate with the appropriate "increasing" of the *numen* man venerates can never be a bribe, nor are they merely a means of preserving a relation of *camaraderie* between devotees and god. The attitude required for true veneration always implies submission of the one who venerates to the will of the object of veneration.

In Christian worship, there is no question of any strengthening of God because, for the Christian, God is all-Sovereign. He is King of them who rule as kings, and Lord of them who rule as lords. The absolute submission of the Christian to God's will is the prime criterion of true worship. In that context, offering of sacrifice to God fulfils the various conditions enumerated earlier —the identification of the offerer with the victim, the accepted authority of the Deity, and the participation by the offerers in the fount of Power that is infinite and outside the normal reach of man, but also binds the co-participants into one body.

For Christians, these conditions exist in the eternal sacrifice of Jesus on the Cross, but have to be appropriated by each Christian so that, as a constituent member of the Body of Christ through baptism, he takes his place in the sacrifice offered ONCE-and-for-ALL by Jesus Christ himself. He must, however, in his individual existence, go through the experience of being crucified with Christ by offering up to God, himself, his soul and his body as a living sacrifice acceptable to God. The eucharistic sacrifice embodies both these aspects. We first present before God the perfect offering of Jesus Christ and, through the merits of that sacrifice, offer ourselves first as represented by our oblation of bread and wine and also by our total act of praise and thanksgiving to God for all the benefits we receive at His hands. Such an approach to God depends on the mediating work of Jesus the true High Priest and is maintained by the work of his representatives, the human priests of the Church.

This dual aspect of the eucharistic sacrifice is not fully appreciated by those who try to distinguish the sacrifice of praise and thanksgiving from the oblation of ourselves to God, at the Eucharist, emphasizing the importance of the former and the utter irrelevance of the latter. But as Brilioth remarks, ". . . all oblation, all giving to God, may be taken as included in the idea of Thanksgiving: for no oblation that man can make has any religious value except as a spontaneous act of thanksgiving. . . . But the deepest religious meaning of the oblation of material gifts is seen in their symbolical significance, as representing that oblation of self which is a necessary part of all living faith. The Christian has in truth but one gift which he can give to God, namely himself; and the eucharist could not be the central act of Christian worship if it did not include and express this idea."[84] Later he adds: "The eucharistic act is sacrificial because it represents and shows forth the one sacrifice, which, being eternal, is beyond the limitations of time and space. The true celebrant is not the human priest, but Christ the Great High-Priest, in the midst of his disciples; . . . The eucharist is the church's supreme act of prayer, the pleading of the one sacrifice, the expression in ritual of the formula which we repeat, often so heedlessly in our prayers: 'through Jesus Christ our Lord', 'for Jesus Christ's sake'. But it is not only an action external to ourselves. In the act of communion we are united with our High-priest, and we enjoy the benefits of his sacrifice; but we are also dedicated to participate in his self-oblation. Here, above all, the elements of sacrifice, fellowship, thanksgiving, and mystery blend with one another."[85]

Canon O. C. Quick makes a similar point when in a discussion of the doctrine of the Eucharist, he notes that in that central rite of the Church, Christians "are made partakers of the life offered for them on Calvary, in order that, in the end, their communion with that life may be fulfilled in the open and glorious vision of their Saviour before the throne of God".[86] He also later observes

K

that the Eucharist is "truly a sacrifice", but it "is also a communion; for the only way in which Christ's sacrifice can avail for us is by making us one with itself".[87] This last remark means, in effect, that we, united with Christ, give ourselves in complete consecration to Him and through Him to the service of God.

Christian Africans can be led to appreciate that the Eucharist is, first of all, the opportunity for the total self-offering of the individual worshipper to God. Second, it is the Christian family meal at which we participate in the Body and Blood of Jesus Christ, and through that communion enter into a new fellowship with our fellow-men. Indeed, for Christians, the Eucharist is an eschatological meal commemorating our delivery through the death of Christ from the bondage of sin and death and pointing to the consummation of all things "till he comes". Our action does not, however, imply a repetition of the death of Christ on Calvary, as has so often been emphasized.[88] It is, as has already been noted, a representation of that sacrifice offered *in illo tempore*, when Jesus Christ suffered under Pontius Pilate. Africans can readily understand this language.

The Mende of Sierra Leone, for example, have a myth which tells of how God at Creation first offered to the man and the woman whom he had created a chicken each, with the definite instruction to offer it back to Him whenever His presence was required to adjudicate and restore good relations between them. So today, before a Mende man or woman utters an imprecatory curse against his fellow Mende man or woman, he first offers God the chicken which God had originally offered to him or her *in illo tempore*, as his opening move. In fact no physical offering is made; but the eternal offering once made by God is recalled and its presence assumed. The symbolic representation of the original chicken is analogous to the Christian anamnesis in regard to its function, but differs from it in essence and, therefore, in its *raison d'être*.

The one is based on a myth and remains mythical, the other has a myth but is founded on the verifiable, historical life and death of Jesus. There is a further aspect of the Mende anamnesis, viz.: that it always stresses a family notion of all Mende people as children of God, and that all the members of that family should live at peace with each other and should, as far as possible, bear no malice against each other. Where the desired *rapport* has been violated, the aggrieved party may take such steps as he thinks fit to seek redress, but only after first gaining the permission of the head of the family. We recall that the communal meal at the cultic sacrifices provides an occasion for enhancing the solidarity of the family. Indeed, it is widely believed among some groups that to eat of the cultic meal whilst bearing a grudge against a fellow-participant would lead to certain death. So, among the Creole of Sierra Leone, for example, at the *Awujɔ* ceremonies all the little suspected feuds are aired and settled. The members of the hunters' societies within the same group also claim that their hunt will be marred if any one member bears ill-will against another. Indeed, they aver that if a member had committed adultery with a fellow-member's wife he would be hit by a stray shot and perhaps be killed. A similar attitude to life accounts for the emphasis on a "cool mind" free from anger among the Nyakyusa.[89]

The African convert to Christianity could thus be led to understand the significance of the interpretation put on the Eucharist by the early Christians that it was a passover meal, this time, the Christian Passover (cf. Exodus 12: 24–34; Deut. 6: 20 ff.; 1 Cor. 5: 7, 10: 16 f.); that Christians, each in their several generations, can enjoy the saving benefit of Christ's death, and that at the Eucharist they become partakers of the propitiating power of the sacrifice that led to that death.[90] This Paschal meal, in the later stages of the history of the Jews, came to suggest a commemoration of "past redemption, of the interposition of God at the beginning of Israel's history; ... this commemoration of the *past* fired the minds of the participants with hopes for the *future*: for a new interposition of Providence which should set them free from their present servitude".[91] The Christian Eucharist does not in fact reproduce the primary elements of the sacrifice of an animal nor the bitter herbs that should be eaten with it. But it maintains the fundamental reference to the redeeming act of God, and holds out the future hope of entering into the Presence of God through the mediating work of Jesus Christ.

This freedom from the servitude of sin, and the eschatological hope, based on our becoming children of God by adoption through baptism, provide an important element in the teaching of the Christian Church which Christian converts in Africa could understand and appropriate. If the Lordship of Christ could be taught in such a way as not only to convince African Christians that Jesus Christ is more powerful than all the minor deities they formerly worshipped, but also to assure them that Christians can be indwelt by Jesus Christ, as St. Paul tells us of himself in Gal. 2: 19 ff., the feeling of despair and frustration which now haunts many an African Christian when life becomes difficult would be removed. They can then readily be led to grasp the truth that has lain behind the attitude representing "the age-long instinct of the Church that the Eucharist or the Lord's Supper is the supreme moment, or opportunity, for our prayers, of whatever kind, in union with His",[92] i.e., Jesus Christ's, supreme self-offering. They can then more truly understand that the Eucharist is a unique sacrifice, participation in which does not permit of participation in sacrifices offered to demons (cf. 1 Cor. 10: 21).

Again, whilst modern physicists and biochemists might frown at the Pauline dictum that eating the Lord's Supper unworthily causes men to fall ill and sometimes die (cf. 1 Cor. 11: 30), African converts to Christianity, who already believe that to eat cultic meals unworthily—with special reference to hostility towards their fellow-men—does lead to sickness and death, will readily appreciate and understand the Pauline remark. Indeed, future African psychologists may yet be able to interpret the power of mind over body in this context. It is worth noting here that in Sierra Leone the older Christians believed that attendance at the Holy Communion called for special preparedness of mind and body.

We are now in a position to postulate certain principles which would guide the adoption of the five-action rite of the African cultic liturgy mentioned earlier, viz.:

(i) That the Eucharist is a *sacrifice* at which we offer first our physical gifts which ultimately symbolize the offering of *ourselves* to God. The physical objects in our case are bread and wine with which may be associated any sums of money we wish to offer to God. These all represent the results of human labour in one form or the other, and so ultimately represent the offerers.

(ii) That these offerings are tokens of our acknowledgement of the Sovereignty of God and of our humble penitence for resisting His will.

(iii) That our gifts, after having been first offered to God by us, are later offered by God to us; but, this time, they have become charged with a new *essence*.

(iv) That as a corollary of our being able to make due offerings acceptable to God, we must seek to be appropriately clean, hence the need for Confession and Absolution. But as the Book of Common Prayer so aptly states it, the worshippers should not only strive to "live in charity with their neighbours", they must also "intend to lead a new life, following the commandments of God, and walking from henceforth in His holy ways".

(All Christians should realize that they belong to a community in which each should first learn to feel a concern for his neighbour.)

(v) That the Eucharist is a communal meal at which we all share, without distinction, in the concorporateness of the Christian family through the Body and Blood of Christ.

(vi) That because the actual sacrifice offered is that of the Body and Blood of Jesus Christ, offered at Calvary, the service should always end with a note of thanksgiving for God's self-offering of Himself in Jesus Christ.

Brief comments are called for at this stage on (i) the change *in essence* of the elements offered up after the Prayer of Consecration, and (ii) the "real presence" of Jesus Christ at the altar.

The latter notion is implicit in the earlier reference to the sacrifice ŋgewɔ is said by the Mende of Sierra Leone to have offered to mankind and which they, in turn, always assume to be present when invoked before they utter a curse on their fellow-men. For the Christian, the sacrifice referred to is that offered on the Cross by Jesus Christ. It is therefore important that African Christians should be taught the doctrine of the real presence at the Eucharist. Equally so, instruction on the change in essence of the eucharistic elements after consecration may be built around the belief that the communal meal, eaten at pagan African rites, may lead to the death of any participant who is in malice with his neighbour because it is no longer ordinary food after it has been offered as a sacrifice.

The Creole of Sierra Leone have a very significant instance of a similar belief, though in a different context. Often, they set food—rice and gravy—on a table at night, particularly after a death, for the deceased to feed on when they visit their homes. This food is, of course, always found intact next morning and eaten up. But care is always taken for it to be eaten cold. In the days when some rice was usually preserved overnight for the children's breakfast, special care was always taken for it to be carefully heated before it was eaten. It is significant that the food left for the dead must be eaten cold. Why are the same people, who strive to ensure that children have no stomach disorders through eating ordinary food cold, anxious to ensure that the special food set for their dead is not heated before consumption? After long and careful enquiries, the writer discovered that it was believed that the dead had touched the food with their spirit hands, now cold in death. So, to heat the food was to remove the touch of the dead; and, because the food had been touched it had become different in essence, though not in form, and had acquired a new potency which prevented the children who partook of it cold from having any stomach disorders.

The Shape of a Probable Liturgy

We can now see the probable shape of a Christian liturgy which will meet the religio-psychological needs of African converts to Christianity. This may be outlined as follows:

I. A recital of the Commandments of God, preferably as expressed in the language of Mark 12: 30 f. The ten commandments may, however, be prescribed on certain days—First Sunday in Advent, all Sundays in Lent, and at the main Eucharistic Service on Easter Day. The *Kyrie* may of course be substituted for the commandments as may seem fit.

The *Non dignus sum* may be introduced here after the Commandments or *Kyrie* to provide the first stage of the healing process—as is usual in the African rites.

II. The Collect, followed by scripture reading—an Old Testament passage, a New Testament lesson or an Epistle, and a Gospel passage.

III. A Sermon.

IV. The Nicene Creed.

V. The Offertory. In view of the fact that there is a strong communal element in all aspects of African life, each worshipper should contribute his own portion of the bread, by placing a wafer into the ciborium as he enters the Church. The bread and wine together with the offering of money will then form a complete oblation made up by the active contributions of those present and participating. These oblations should be offered up publicly.

VI. A litany, constructed on the pattern of the deacon's litany in the Early Church, with special reference to the situations of the living members and at the same time making mention of the dead—both Christian and non-Christian.

VII. The Canon of the Mass providing for the *Memento* for the living, and the *Quam Oblationem*; a Prayer of Consecration, followed by an offering up of the sacrifice of the worshippers in union with the true sacrifice of Christ; the *Memento* for the Dead; the *Agnus Dei*.

VIII. The General Confession followed by an Absolution, or the Prayer of Humble Access—to signify the usual washing which precedes the eating of the communal meal.

IX. The Communion of Priest and People.

X. A Prayer of Thanksgiving followed by the *Gloria in*

Excelsis to provide a Christian equivalent of the usual joyful note which usually marks the end of the African rites.

XI. A final dismissal, which should give the communicants that sense of release and restoration which the propitiatory rites give the Africans and at the same time engender that feeling of *camaraderie* which is enhanced by the joyfulness of the last stages of the African rites. In addition, an attempt should be made to stress the need for a careful observance of the moral code of the community as pre-scribed and guarded by the Christian faith to provide a Christian counterpart to the demands and admonitions of cultic worship among pagan Africans. Such a dismissal should end on a sort of martial note which emphasizes the essential qualities of sound Christian living. So, we would suggest a form of dismissal in language akin to the words proposed in the Deposited Prayer Book of 1928, at the end of the Alternative Order of Confirmation, viz.: "Go forth into the world in peace; be of good courage; hold fast that which is good; render to no man evil for evil; strengthen the fainthearted; support the weak; help the afflicted; honour all men; love and serve the Lord, rejoicing in the power of the Holy Spirit;

> And the blessing of God Almighty, the Father, the Son, and the Holy Ghost, be upon you, and remain with you for ever."

Basic to this approach to the Eucharist must lie the funda-mental notion that it offers spiritual health and healing. Our sinful bodies can "be made clean by Christ's Body" and "our souls washed through His most precious Blood". This healing aspect of the Eucharist was recognized by the Early Church. Ignatius called it the "medicine of immortality".[93] Unlike the African propitiatory rites, however, the Eucharist is not a clinic which meets only when there are cases of physical illness. The Christian has to contend with spiritual forces all the time, and must, therefore, be always on the alert, ready to resist sin, and, more determinedly, to cultivate peace within the Christian brotherhood. So he must learn to make frequent communions, both to stabilize his own faith and to strengthen the communal bond. This aspect needs to be emphasized within the African context. Ignatius understood the value of such comings-together and therefore advised the Ephesians to "meet more frequently to celebrate God's Eucharist and to offer praise". He goes on, "For, when you meet frequently in the same place, the forces of Satan are overthrown, and his baneful influence is neutralized by the unanimity of your faith. Peace is a precious thing: it puts an end to every war waged by heavenly or earthly enemies".[94]

We would also stress that the Africans' practice of making confessions in their pagan situation ought to be encouraged when they become Christians. Such confessions would, however, be voluntary and would never be extracted by force, as sometimes is the case in pagan communities. Instead, the African Christian should be helped to appreciate the blessings of the Sacrament of Penance and the concomitant spiritual release which follows the Absolution and forgiveness which it offers to penitents.[95]

Instruction on the Church's ministry of healing should also be carefully organized in order to offset the authority vested in pagan cultic priests, and whenever possible the Church should seek to establish doctor-priest teams. The spiritual ingredients of the pagan healing rites will thus be provided when the sick receive medical treatment as well as the spiritual benefits of Christian Confession and Absolution.[96]

The new life born of new hope will now be firmly anchored in Jesus Christ. For, as Dr. W. J. T. Kimber so aptly says, "New life (during treatment) brings with it a sense of joy and peace and an abiding sense of the reality and presence of God", when religious healing rites and the ministration of the Eucharist are associated with medical attention.[97]

When the Eucharistic Sacrifice has become the central act of worship of every African Christian, it would also cater for all the social and emotional needs which demanded the pagan sacrifices. Here again, the example of the Early Church provides a pattern for the Church in Africa. As we have pointed out, commemorations of the dead formed a significant part of their worship. In addition, Christian festivals were instituted to displace pagan festal days, thus offering Christians from a pagan background opportunities of offering the Sacrifice of Christ on the days when their heathen compatriots celebrated a pagan festival with sacrifice of one form or the other. A good instance of this is the institution of the *Major Litania* on April 25, when the Church went out in procession to provide a Christian counterpart to the pagan festival of *Robigalia*.[98] Similar practices can be instituted in Africa by the establishment of Christian festivals to replace important national pagan festivals like the *Hɔmɔwa*, the *Adwera* and the *Adae* in Ghana; such a step would demonstrate that the Church lives to "take" over "the religious capital of the natural man", and to sanctify it.[99] To this end, we would urge that an African Calendar should be carefully designed to cater for the needs of the African situation.[100] By this means, Christians in Africa would be encouraged to resort to the Church for all their spiritual needs; their conversion would be complete and their practice of the Faith more genuine.

Acceptance of these suggestions naturally depends on the theological interpretation of the functions of the Christian minister. Is he a sacrifice-offering priest or not? As an Anglican priest who fully accepts the doctrine of a sacrificing priesthood, the writer is firmly convinced that only a sacerdotal ministry can meet the emotional and spiritual demands of the African if he is to feel at home in the Christian family, both in private and, especially, on festal occasions. Only a priest can bring the penitent African Christian the absolution, forgiveness and hope which he would expect on being converted to Christianity; only a priest can lead him to offer up to God the sacrifice without which he would not feel he could approach the altar of God.[101] Only a Christian priest can provide for the African convert to Christianity the complete release from anxiety, worry and depression which he formerly sought at the cultic shrines, because, as a Christian, he comes completely under the Holy Spirit of God from whom we receive a new life. In the language of a former Bishop of Truro, the Holy Spirit confers on the Christian, "release from sin, release from neurosis, releases from stress, dryness and hardening, and release of latent powers".[102]

Here we think we are likely to trigger off Dr. Baeta's "theological battle-royal",[103] which we have so far striven to avoid. The risk of such a conflict is quite great, since most of the Churches of the historic tradition which exist in Africa stem from the Reformed traditions. But the problem will have to be faced sooner or later. It is significant that Dr. Idowu, whilst observing that "not a few of the divinities" of the Yoruba were the product of the priests, acting on the impulse of certain motives, some detrimental to the people, also states that the people "who *must* worship" have followed the leadership of the priests. Indeed, he deplores the fact that no "prophets" arose to keep Yoruba religion within the framework of its "primitive purity". Derogatory as these comments may sound, they do indicate the place and influence of the Yoruba priests within their community.[104] This type of influence wielded by the priests on their society is not peculiar to the Yoruba. It is widespread. Even when there are found communities in which professional priests are not appointed, the oldest member of the tribe, the family or the clan, takes the place of the priest.

The importance of the role of the sacerdotal ministry is clearly evident in all the African cultic rites. It is a major factor in African life. Wherever one goes it is seen to be the coping-stone of tribal life.

"FAITH IS BELIEVING OBEDIENCE." This definition of Faith is as true of pagan religious thinking as it is of Christian teaching. The faith which pagan Africans evince in the cultic spirits and the ancestors is indicative of their willingness to submit to the will of spirits they revere. Whilst it is true to say that the worship of the pagan cults is built around the principle of "give and take", it must also be said that pagan life in Africa is geared to an unreserved obedience to the will of the spirit or spirits invoked. If Christians could become truly alive to this fact, ways and means could be found to establish in African converts to Christianity a richer relation with the God of Jesus Christ. In Christian thinking, the unreserved submission of our wills to God demands a complete surrender of our natural desires and a dedication of our entire selves to the service of God. Only so can the Holy Spirit of God tabernacle in our lives and give us the true life—the life in Christ. It should, therefore, be stressed that "Christianity is the only religion which really faces the problem of sin and offers to provide a remedy; it is the one faith which gives an adequate place to personality, both human and divine; whilst its great ideals of service, purity, humility, holiness, the recognition of the equal rights of all men, are not to be found elsewhere, save when there has been definite borrowing from it."[1] Only then will African Christians more readily respond to Christian evangelistic appeals and respond without any reservations.

The change of emphasis advocated in this work will naturally provoke discussion, especially in circles which would be inclined to reject our approach to the African situation. In any case, our suggestions will demand a new outlook among African Church leaders and foreign missionaries. The vast majority of foreign missionaries operating in Africa naturally belong to groups which are opposed to priestcraft on grounds of which they are not often sure, and which, in fact, are unrelated to the African situation. On the other hand, in Africa, priestcraft and, with it, confession, absolution and sacrifice are deeply ingrained in the life-setting and thought of the peoples. These factors, as has so often been noted, constitute the woof and warp of life in Africa. Christian leaders of today must therefore not reject these attitudes off-hand because they do not quite fit into a pattern which developed out of a period of tension in Europe and the United States of America several centuries ago. In any case, the debates are irrelevant to the African situation. Meanwhile we would stress that Christianity has so far manifested a unique capacity for "adjusting itself to new conditions".[2]

Our suggestions, however, call for a new pattern of training of the ministry in Africa.[3] This is the aim of Dr. Sundkler's important book, *The Christian Ministry in Africa*. Signs of a welcome change are already manifest in East Africa, judging from the recently published report on *Training for the Ministry in East Africa*. In West Africa, Fourah Bay College has instituted a course which provides opportunities for teachers and students to examine the traditional beliefs and practices of Africans, with a view to discovering which of these elements may be consecrated to the service of Christianity and which are to be rejected if Christianity is to have a firm foothold in this great continent. Courses in African Religions are also provided in the other university institutions in West Africa. Much work has yet to be done by African Christians, theologians and laymen alike, before a clear picture can emerge. But the signs of change are promising.[4]

Once it is realized that "it is not necessary" for the African to "become detribalized to become a Christian, the Christianization of pagan customs and beliefs would seem to be the most natural and reasonable means of re-establishing the indigenous culture on the basis of a higher scale of spiritual values and transcendent realities, thereby avoiding the inevitable consequences that follow when the spiritual dynamic of a society is allowed to disintegrate".[5] Of course, necessary safeguards must be provided to avoid any syncretism. But the Church in Africa must humbly seek to listen to the call of God in Jesus Christ who said:

"I came that men may have life, and may have it in all its fullness" (John 10: 10. N.E.B.).

If we are patient enough to distil from the corpus of African traditional beliefs and practices such factors as are consonant with Christianity, we shall ultimately redeem them unto the obedience of Christ.

May the Church in Africa be the vehicle of abundant life for all Africans.

NOTES

Chapter 1

1. Bengt Sundkler, *Bantu Prophets in South Africa*, 2nd ed., London, 1961, p. 281.

2. Cf. p. 44 ff. above for a fuller discussion of this topic.

3. Fr. Placide Tempels, *Bantu Philosophy*, *Présence Africaine*, E.T. Paris, 1959, p. 65.

4. Cf. p. 117 f. above.

5. Edwin Smith, *African Ideas of God*, London, 1950, p. 282 footnote. Fr. Placide Tempels makes the important comment that "The destruction of life is a conspiracy against the Divine Plan; and the *muntu* knows that such destruction is, above all else, ontological sacrilege; that it is for that reason immoral and therefore unjust" (*op. cit.*, p. 79).

6. Margaret Field, *Search for Security*, London, 1960, p. 48.

7. Cf. Jomo Kenyatta, *Facing Mt. Kenya*, Mercury Books, London, 1961, p. 236.

8. J. Schlenker, *A Collection of Temne Traditions, Fables and Proverbs*, London, 1861, pp. 25–29.

9. Eva Meyerowitz, *The Divine Kingship in Ghana and Ancient Egypt*, London, 1960, p. 105 f.

10. Cf. Fr. Placide Tempels, *op. cit.*, p. 32.

11. *Ibidem.*

12. *Sierra Leone Bulletin of Religion*, Vol. 4, No. 2, 1962, p. 44. Article on "The Dogma of Super-Size I", by Harry Sawyerr.

13. E. B. Idowu, *Olodumare*, London, 1962, p. 173 f.

14. *Ibidem*, p. 77.

15. *Ibidem*, p. 177.

16. *Ibidem*, p. 178.

17. *Ibidem*, p. 182.

18. *Ibidem*, p. 171.

19. *Odu* No. 2, article by Bradbury on *Ehi*.

20. M. Fortes, *Oedipus and Job*, Cambridge, 1959, Cap. VI.

21. Cf. K. A. Busia in Daryll Forde, *African Worlds*, London, 1954, p. 191 f.; Fr. Placide Tempels, *op. cit.*, p. 39.

22. Cf. R. S. Rattray, *Ashanti*, Oxford, 1923, p. 263; Eva Meyerowitz, *The Sacred State of the Akan*, London, 1951, p. 199.

23. Cf. C. Northcote Thomas, *Law and Custom of the Temne and other tribes*, London, 1916, p. 76.

24. P. Amaury Talbot, *Some Nigerian Fertility Cults*, London, 1927, pp. 33 f., 124.

25. Cf. R. S. Rattray, *op. cit.*, p. 214; Eva Meyerowitz, *The Akan of Ghana*, London, 1958, p. 31.

26. K. A. Busia, *The Position of the Chief in the Modern System of Ashanti*, London, 1958, p. 134, and Appendix III.

27. P. Amaury Talbot, *Some Nigerian Fertility Cults*, London, 1927, p. 12.

28. Efraim Andersson, *Messianic Popular Movements in the Lower Congo*, Uppsala, 1958, p. 14.

29. E. B. Idowu, *op. cit.*, p. 149 f.

30. Cf. May M. Edel, *The Chiga of Western Uganda*, New York, 1957, p. 130 f.; Kenneth Little, *The Mende of Sierra Leone*, 1st edn. London, 1951, p. 192 f.; J. R. Wilson-Haffenden, *The Red Men of Nigeria*, London, 1930, p. 289.

31. Cf. *Sierra Leone Bulletin of Religion*, Vol. 5, No. 2, December 1963, article on *Disɔŋ*, by Harry Sawyerr and A. W. Sawyerr; Kenneth Little, *op. cit.*, p. 138, note 3.

32. Cf. Camara Laye, *The African Child*, Fontana Books, London, 1954, p. 104; cf. pp. 82 ff., 94; Colin Turnbull, *op. cit.*, Cap. 4, 9.

33. Cf. Mary Kingsley, *Travels in West Africa*, London, 1897, p. 544 f.

34. For a good discussion of Mother Earth, see Mircea Eliade, *Myths, Dreams and Mysteries*, E.T. London, 1960, Cap. VII.

35. J. V. Taylor, *Primal Vision*, London, 1963, p. 196.

36. Cf. *ibidem*, p. 83.

37. *Sierra Leone Bulletin of Religion* No. 1, 1959, article on "Sacrificial Rituals in Sierra Leone", p. 2, by Harry Sawyerr.

38. Cf. Ulli Beier, *A Year of Sacred Festivals*, a Nigeria Magazine Production, Lagos, 1959, p. 26.

39. Cf. *Sierra Leone Bulletin of Religion*, Vol. 5, No. 2, December 1963, article on *Disɔŋ*, by Harry Sawyerr and A. W. Sawyerr.

40. *Al-Lat* is an old Arabian goddess, found in Nabatean and Palmyran inscriptions and later worshipped by various Bedouin tribes. An oath by *Al-Lat* is frequently found in the poets (cf. *Shorter Encyclopaedia of Islam*, by H. A. R. Gibb and J. M. Kramers, Leiden and London,

1953, p. 287); C. M. Doughty tells of a "bethel-stone" of black granite rock known as *el-Lata*, "which is venus of the Arabs", according to Herodotus (*Travels in Arabia Deserta*, Vol. II, London, 1921, p. 516). The Temne oath-taking formula given by one reliable informant before a court case is opened is interpreted by him as pointing to *Al-Lat*.

(*The witness first looks for a suitable spot in the court; turns to the east and says*):

"Lɔ-ɔ-n-ta! Lɔ-ɔ-n-ta! i lafte ro torɔŋ; i tola kuru; i nesa tesuɛnla; i tola kuru; Lɔ-ɔ-n-ta! Lɔ-ɔ-n-ta! kara Bai; Lɔ-ɔ-ɔ-n-ta!" i.e., "I turn to the East, I pay homage, I fear the lions, I pay homage to *Lat* and pay homage to the monarch of the lions".

(I am grateful to Mr. Ahmadu Wurie, formerly Minister of the Interior in Sierra Leone, for permission to use this information from a talk he gave at the Easter Vacation Course for Clergy and Ministers run by the Department of Theology of Fourah Bay College, in March 1962.)

41. E. Evans-Pritchard, *Neuer Religion*, London, 1956, p. 8 f.; Edwin Smith, *op. cit.*, p. 261; cf. R. T. Parsons, *Religion in an African Society*, Brill, Leiden, 1964, p. 163; Harry Sawyerr in *Sierra Leone Bulletin of Religion*, Vol. 3, No. 2, 1961, p. 44.

42. J. V. Taylor, *op. cit.*, p. 84 *et passim*.

43. R. T. Parsons, *op. cit.*, p. 163.

44. W. G. de Lara Wilson, *William Vincent Lucas*, London, 1950, p. 41.

45. Cf. pp. 15, 25.

46. Cf. *Sierra Leone Bulletin of Religion*, Vol. 6, No. 1, June 1964, article on "Limba Swears", by Ruth Finegan; *Sierra Leone Studies*, N.S. No. 13, June 1960, p. 32, article on "The Temne Ansasa", by J. Littlejohn; cf. Fr. Jarrett-Kerr, *African Pulse*, London, 1960, Cap. 2, 5.

Fr. Jarrett-Kerr's description of the African situation is significant; particularly so, as he tries to enter into the "socio-psychological" (and "spiritual") factors (p. 39) that influence the reactions of Africans. Much work is still waiting to be done for us to be able to grasp the role of these factors in the behaviour of the African, studied as a normal human being and not merely as an anthropological phenomenon of high museum-piece value.

Chapter 2

1. Charles Gore (ed.), *Lux Mundi*, 10th ed., London, 1904, p. 71; cf. Hugo Rahner, *Greek Myths and Christian Mystery*, Eng. trans., London, 1963, p. 95.

2. Jackson and Lake, *The Beginnings of Christianity*, Vol. IV, p. 202, notes *ad loc.*

3. Philip Carrington, *The Primitive Christian Catechism*, Cambridge, 1940; cf. especially, Tables I, II, III; cf. E. G. Selwyn, *I Peter*, London, 1947, Essay II, pp. 365–465.

4. For *glory* as a numinous word, cf. E. G. Selwyn, *op. cit.*, p. 256.

5. Sir William Ramsay thinks that baptism is the seal "of turning to the Lord" (cf. 1 Thess. 1:9) even though "the State of mind called πιστεύειν (to believe), sometimes advanced no farther than intellectual assent and emotional impression . . ." (*The Teachings of St. Paul in terms of the Present Day*, London, 1913, p. 446).

6. Cf. G. Milligan, *Thessalonians*, London, 1908, Intro., p. xxxiii f., p. 48 f., notes to IV: 3.

7. Cf. J. F. Hort, in *Journal of Theological Studies*, Vol. III, 1902, p. 594 ff., article on ΕΥΧΑΡΙΣΤΙΑ–ΕΥΧΑΡΙΣΤΕΙΝ.

8. Cf. Roland Allen, *Missionary Methods: St. Paul's or Ours?* London, 1959 (reprint), p. 113.

9. *Ibidem*, p. 115.

10. *Ibidem*, p. 114 f.

11. Cf. Bengt Sundkler, *Bantu Prophets in South Africa*, 2nd ed., London, 1961, *passim.*

12. Godfrey Phillips, *The Old Testament in the World Church*, London, 1942, p. 6. T. W. Manson of course has argued that 1 Thessalonians was written after 2 Thessalonians, but that argument does not upset our present use of the letter (cf. *Studies in the Gospels and Epistles* (ed. M. Black), Manchester University Press, 1962, Cap. 14).

13. *Ibidem*, pp. 11, 125 f.

14. *Ibidem*, p. 8.

15. *Ibidem*, p. 120.

16. *Ibidem*.

17. *Ibidem*, Part IV, Cap. II.

18. Bengt Sundkler, *The Christian Ministry in Africa*, London, 1960, p. 281.

19. *Ibidem*, p. 282.

20. *Ibidem*, p. 285.

21. *Ibidem*, p. 286.

22. G. Phillips, *op. cit.*, p. 95.

23. *Ibidem*, p. 138.

24. *Ibidem*, p. 12 f.

25. *Ibidem*, p. 117.

26. *Ibidem*, p. 13.

27. Bengt Sundkler, *The Christian Ministry in Africa*, p. 282.

28. Cf. J. Schlenker, *op. cit.*, pp. 15–21.

29. E. B. Idowu, *op. cit.*, Cap. 3.

30. *Ibidem*, p. 21.

31. *Ibidem*, p. 21.

32. *Ibidem*, p. 71, cf. p. 21.

33. Fela Sowande, IFA, Lagos, pp. 35, 39 ff., cf. p. 16.

34. *Ibidem*, pp. 38, 40 ff.

35. *Ibidem*, p. 37 f.

36. *Ibidem*, p. 78, cf. Fela Sowande, *op. cit.*, p. 40.

37. Cf. p. 17 f. below.

38. Cf. Daryll Forde, *African Worlds*, p. 192; R. S. Rattray, *Ashanti Proverbs*, pp. 20–22; E. B. Idowu, *op. cit.*, p. 22; Hans Abrahamsson, *The Origin of Death*, Studia Ethnographia Uppsalensia III, Eng. edition, London, 1951, p. 73.

39. E. B. Idowu, *op. cit.*, p. 56.

40. *Ibidem*, p. 47.

41. *Ibidem*, p. 46.

42. Fela Sowande, *op. cit.*, p. 53; cf. pp. 45–53.

43. Archetypal events of course played a similar role in the religion of the Hebrews, but, in their case, the events were historical—the call of Abraham, the institution of the covenant of circumcision, the Exodus, the crossing of the Red Sea, the giving of the Sinai covenant, the settlement in Canaan. So sacred were the events of the Exodus, the crossing of the Red Sea and the Sinaitic covenant that the prescription that proselytes were to undergo circumcision, baptism and sacrifice was interpreted to be a "re-enactment of the exodus and the pilgrimage ensuing on it, with the gift of the Torah as the climax" (D. Daube, *The New Testament and Rabbinic Judaism*, London, 1956, p. 131). The same principle applies to the Christian religion. Here, in particular, the death of Jesus Christ and the sacrifice on the cross are described as having taken place *once* and *once* only (ἐφάπαξ) (see Romans 6: 10, Hebrews 7: 27). So, too, the repetition of the eucharistic rite is said by St. Paul to be a proclamation of the death of Jesus "until He comes" (1 Cor. 11: 26); the archetypal events are, however, historical; Jesus "suffered under Pontius Pilate"; died and was buried, but God raised Him from the dead.

44. See G. E. Wright, *God who Acts*, London, 1952, *imp.* Cap. 1, 2;

Th. C. Vriezen, *An Outline of Old Testament Theology*, Oxford, 1958, pp. 136–47, Cap. VII.

45. E. B. Idowu, *op. cit.*, p. 190.

46. *Ibidem*, p. 150.

47. Trumbull, *Blood-Covenant*, Edinburgh, 1887; Lord Lugard used the blood-covenant to establish peace with several East African tribes (cf. Margery Perham and Mary Bull, *The Diaries of Lord Lugard*, London, 1959, 3 vols.; Vol. I, pp. 289, 301, 344, 416; Vol. II, p. 226).

48. See *Vetus Testamentum*, Vol. IX, No. 1, 1959, p. 7.

49. See J. B. Danquah, *op. cit.*, pp. 20, 25; cf. pp. 55, 101, 125.

50. Cf. Eva Meyerowitz, *The Divine Kingship in Ghana and Ancient Egypt*, p. 28 f.

51. Eva Meyerowitz, *The Divine Kingship in Ghana and Ancient Egypt*, p. 111; cf. p. 200 for a description of the rite by which the predecessor king is transfigured at Takyiman. Mrs. Meyerowitz elsewhere observes that "the sun-god cult was exclusively an ancestor-cult in the royal line" (*ibidem*, p. 88).

52. Eva Meyerowitz, *The Sacred State of the Akan*, p. 57 and footnote.

53. Eva Meyerowitz, *The Akan of Ghana*, p. 85 f.

54. E. B. Idowu, *op. cit.*, p. 15.

55. *Ibidem*, p. 23.

56. *Ibidem*, p. 24.

57. *Ibidem*, p. 22; J. B. Danquah propounds a doctrine of an Akan Messiah based on the deification of the *Opanyim* after his death (*op. cit.*, p. 120 ff.); for a discussion of this doctrine see pp. 102–105. According to Sowande, *Modakeke* was king of the original *Ile-Ife* according to the *Odu* (*op. cit.*, p. 51).

58. Samuel Johnson, *A History of the Yorubas*, London, 1921, p. 38.

59. Cf. J. B. Danquah, *op. cit.*, p. 120 ff.

60. J. Wilson-Haffenden, *op. cit.*, p. 295.

61. Th. C. Vriezen, *op. cit.*, p. 145 f.; cf. pp. 200, 220; but cf. J. Schoeps, *Paul*, Eng. trans., London, 1961, p. 90 f. and footnote 4.

62. Cf. Barnabas Lindbars, *New Testament Apocalyptic*, London, 1961, p. 196; 247–50.

63. Cf. C. K. Barrett, *Romans*, London, 1957, p. 88 f.

64. W. Robertson Nicol, *The Expositor's Greek Testament*, New York, Vol. II, Part II (*Romans*, by James Denney), p. 668; notes on 9: 33. Cf. also *Journal of Theological Studies*, New Series, Vol. VI, Part I, April 1955, p. 82 f., article by G. R. Driver on *Two Misunderstood Passages of the Old Testament*, Is. 8: 11–14, Jer. 6: 27–30.

65. See Fleming James, *Personalities of the Old Testament*, London, 1958, p. 253 f.

66. F. J. Leenhardt, *Romans*, English translation, London, 1962, p. 272; cf. Barnabas Lindbars, *op. cit.*, pp. 163, 175–81.

67. C. H. Dodd, *According to the Scriptures*, London, 1952, p. 42.

68. C. K. Barrett, *op. cit.*, p. 194; cf. F. J. Leenhardt, *op. cit.*, p. 263 footnote.

69. Ethelbert Stauffer, *New Testament Theology*, English translation, London, 1955, p. 224; cf. Barnabas Lindbars, *op. cit.*, p. 246.

70. *Ibidem.*

71. Cf. Notes 9 and 10 below.

72. Cf. Th. C. Vriezen, *op. cit.*, Chapters 7, 8, 9. Vriezen's comments on the place of the Old Testament for Gentile Christians deserve notice here. He writes:
"For the Gentile Christian world from which the world-wide Church sprang, the preaching of the Gospel was and remained the central element, as the preaching of the risen and glorified Lord, Jesus Christ, the Saviour of the world. The message of His life and work, as recorded in the Gospels, became the starting-point and foundation of faith and life. The Old Testament, it is true, was also accepted as the Word of God and was recognized as canonical, but in fact, as compared with the apostolic witness, to Jesus Christ, it fell into the background (though psychologically rather than theologically)" (*op. cit.*, p. 5); and again: "A Christian theology which clings to the revelatory character of the Gospel and recognizes Jesus Christ as its Lord and Saviour cannot but maintain the revelatory character of the Old Testament, not only because He has accepted this Old Testament as revelation of God, and because His preaching is inconceivable without the Old Testament message concerning God, but especially because Christ's Messianic office cannot be confessed and maintained without the Old Testament" (*ibidem*, p. 9).

73. Dr. J. O. Lucas interprets *Olodumare* to mean, "The Chief or the Exalted One to whom I must go or return" (J. O. Lucas, *The Religion of the Yoruba*, Lagos, 1948, p. 42).

Dr. Idowu adds a third name *Olofin-Orun*, i.e., "The Supreme Sovereign Ruler who is in heaven" (*op. cit.*, p. 36; cf. the whole of Cap. 4).

Chapter 3

1. W. L. Carrington, *Psychology, Religion and Human Need*, London, 1957, p. 308.

2. Cf. William Nicholls, *Revelation in Christ*, London, 1958, p. 114.

3. Cf. A. E. Taylor, *The Faith of a Moralist*, London, 1937, Series I, Cap. VI.

4. L. S. Thornton, *Christ and the Church*, London, 1956, p. 26; cf. D. Daube, *The New Testament and Rabbinic Judaism*, London, 1956, Cap. 6.

5. Cf. J. Pedersen, *Israel I–II*, London, 1926, pp. 411–52, on *Sin and Curse, Israel III–IV*, London, 1953, p. 620 f.; C. H. Dodd, *Romans*, London, 1954, p. 134; G. B. Caird, *Principalities and Powers*, Oxford, 1956, p. 77.

6. Cf. W. L. Carrington, *op. cit.*, p. 68 f.; Lowther Clarke, *Liturgy and Worship*, London, 1950, p. 28, where he says: "True Christian Worship . . . is neither a formless ecstasy nor a dry 'parade-service', but a consecration of all our faculties to His [i.e., God's] Glory."

7. William Nicholls, *op. cit.*, p. 130.

8. *Ibidem*; cf. L. S. Thornton, *Revelation and the Modern World*, London, 1950, Cap. III (i–iv).

9. *Survey of the Training of the Ministry in Africa*, Part III, London and New York, 1954, p. 46.

10. William Nicholls, *op. cit.*, p. 130 f.

11. Cf. *The Times*, London, leading article for September 14, 1955, on *Evangelising*; C. W. J. Bowles, *The Many Fundamentalisms*, London, 1958.

12. Julian Huxley suggests that "it took over a thousand million years for primeval life to generate man", and that a period of "half-million or so years" has elapsed from the appearance of the first Hominidae (*Man in the Modern World* (Mentor Book), New York, 1960, p. 143). Alan Watts more extravagantly professes that "Homo sapiens has probably inhabited this earth for something like a million years . . ." (*Myth and Ritual in Christianity*, London and New York, 1959, p. 14).

13. *Fundamentalism*, p. 24; letter by Dr. Mervyn Stockwood. *The Times* compiled the correspondence it published in 1955 into a pamphlet with the title, *Fundamentalism, A Religious Problem*. Letters to *The Times* and a leading article, London, 1955. Cf. also, letters by G. T. Manley, p. 14; Lionel Gough, p. 20; and Dr. A. M. Ramsey (then Bishop of Durham), p. 7; Oliver Stott, p. 22. Cf. A. E. Taylor, *op. cit.*, Series II, Cap. II.

14. *Ibidem*, p. 27; letter by L. John Collins.

15. Cf. *Survey of the Training of the Ministry in Africa*, Part I, London and New York, 1950, p. 44.

16. *Fundamentalism*, p. 10; letter by J. P. Lewis; cf. L. S. Thornton, *Revelation and the Modern World*, Cap. III (IV–IX).

17. *Ibidem*, p. 11; letter by the Bishop of Southwell.

18. Letter to *The Times*, London, July 1, 1954, by the Rev. E. A. Berrisford. The following comment may also be mentioned: "... Africa is increasingly aware of the keen evangelism of mission groups lacking any strong church sense and in sharp denunciation of existing Churches", *World Christian Handbook*, 1952 edition, London, p. 22.

19. Eva Meyerowitz, *The Sacred State of the Akan*, p. 121, cf. p. 117. Barbara Ward, commenting on the proliferation of pagan shrines in Ghana after World War II, suggests that the old gods having proved incapable of dealing with the contemporary situation, Ghanaians resorted to the importation and creation of new ones (cf. *Africa*, Vol. XXVI, No. 1, 1956, pp. 47–60).

20. K. A. Busia, *Social Survey of Sekondi-Takoradi*, London, 1950, p. 79 ff.

21. M. J. Field, *Religion and Medicine of the Ga People*, Accra and London, 1937, p. 131 f.; cf. footnote 1, p. 132.

22. Cf. Norman Pittenger, *The Word Incarnate*, New York, 1959, p. 17.

23. *International Review of Missions*, Vol. XLV, No. 180, October, 1956, p. 395.

24. Cf. K. A. Busia, *The Position of the Chief in the Modern Political System of Ashanti*, pp. 12, 21, 100; T. O. Elias, *The Nature of African Customary Law*, Manchester, 1956, pp. 19, 98; L. P. Mair, *Chieftainship in Modern Africa* in *Africa*, Vol. IX, 1936; S. Johnson, *A History of the Yorubas*, London, 1921, p. 70.

25. Max Gluckmann has observed that "Witchcraft as a theory of causation, is concerned with the singularity of misfortune" (*Custom and Conflict in Africa*, Oxford, 1955, p. 83, cf. p. 58).

26. Leonard Hodgson, *For Faith and Freedom*, 2 vols., Oxford, 1956 and 1957. Vol. I, p. 82, cf. Vol. II, p. 54.

27. Margaret J. Field, *Search for Security*, London, 1960, p. 35 ff.; H. Debrunner, *Witchcraft in Ghana*, Kumasi, 1959, p. 69.

28. Placide Tempels, *op. cit.*, p. 19.

29. *Ibidem*.

30. *Ibidem*.

31. Cf. *ibidem*, p. 23.

32. H. Debrunner, *op. cit.*, p. 68.

33. *Ibidem*, p. 69.

34. E. B. Idowu, *op. cit.*, pp. 143, 211.

35. Cf. S. G. Williamson, *Akan Religion and the Christian Faith*, edited by Kwesi Dickson, Accra, 1965, Cap. VIII.

36. *The Church*, World Council of Churches, Faith and Order Commission Papers No. 7, London, 1951, p. 70.

37. The Bidding Prayer of the *1604 Canons of the Church of England*, Canon 55; cf. The Homily for Whitsunday in which it is said that "the true Church is an universal congregation or fellowship of God's faithful and elect people ..." (*The Homilies*, Oxford, 1859, p. 462); cf. Eric Mascall, *Christ, the Christian and the Church*, London, 1946, pp. 118–24; Cerfaux, *The Church in the Theology of St. Paul*, New York, 1959, Cap. V, VI.

38. *Survey of the Training of the Ministry in Africa*, Part III, p. 38; cf. W. Visser 't Hooft (ed.), *The New Delhi Report*, London, 1962, pp. 188–95.

39. Arnold Toynbee, *A Study of History*, 6 vols., Vol. I, second ed., London, 1935, p. 211; cf. J. W. C. Wand, *The Church, its Nature, Structure and Function*, London, 1949, pp. 14–20.

40. Adopting the passive rendering of τοῦ ... πληρουμένου following Armitage Robinson, *St. Paul's Epistle to the Ephesians*, second ed., London, 1909, p. 152; cf. B. F. Westcott, *The Epistles of St. John*, London, 1892, p. 32 footnote; Louis Bouyer, *Life and Liturgy*, London, 1956, p. 107. For another rendering based on the Middle Voice, see E. F. Scott, *Moffatt's Commentary, Colossians, Philemon and Ephesians*, London, 1948, p. 159 f.; L. S. Thornton, *The Common Life in the Body of Christ*, third ed., London, 1950, p. 306, footnote 2.

41. J. W. C. Wand, *New Testament Letters*, London, 1946, p. 114.

42. See William Nicholls, *op. cit.*, p. 129 f.; H. W. Robinson, *Redemption and Revelation*, London, 1942, pp. 87–92.

43. William Nicholls, *op. cit.*, p. 130.

44. J. Danielou, *The Lord of History*, London, 1959, p. 26.

45. *Ibidem*, p. 25.

46. Cf. J. V. Taylor, *op. cit.*, pp. 21–25.

47. Thomas Hodgkin, *Nationalism in Colonial Africa*, London, 1956, p. 108. For a fuller discussion see Bengt Sundkler, *Bantu Prophets in South Africa*, p. 278 ff.

48. *International Review of Missions*, Vol. XLIV, No. 175, p. 298, article on "The Christian Church and African Heritage". The Wolofs

of Gambia are said to be, generally speaking, a monogamous group.

49. *Ibidem*, p. 299.

50. The (Sunday) *Observer*, London, March 20, 1960.

51. Cf. G. Parrinder, *West African Religion*, London, 1961, p. 106; J. V. Taylor, *op. cit.* p. 111.

52. Cf. Sherwin Bailey, *The Mystery of Love and Marriage*, London, 1952, Cap. III. We recall that in the Old Testament, adultery and idolatry are identified, cf. Hosea 1–6; Ezekiel 23, 24, 30, 33.

53. J. Dawley (ed.), *Anglican Congress 1954*, London, 1955, p. 177; cf. Sherwin Bailey, *op. cit.*, Cap. II, IV, VII.

54. Margaret Trowell, *African Tapestry*, London, 1957, p. 126.

55. G. Parrinder, *op. cit.*, p. 62 f.

56. Cf. E. B. Idowu, *op. cit.*, p. 196; P. Amaury Talbot, *Tribes of Southern Nigeria*, Oxford, 1926, 4 vols., Vol. II, p. 273.

57. See J. B. Danquah, *The Akan Doctrine of God*, London, 1944, pp. 82 f., 91 f.; Eva Meyerowitz, *The Akan of Ghana*, p. 96.

58. Bengt Sundkler, *The Christian Ministry in Africa*, p. 306.

59. Cf. Eva Meyerowitz, *The Sacred State of the Akan*, pp. 65–68; cf. Monica Wilson, *Communal Rituals of the Nyakyusa*, London, 1959, p. 151; cf. also notes 50–60 of Chapter II.

60. *Ibidem*; cf. J. V. Taylor, *op. cit.*, p. 96 f.

61. Colin Turnbull, *op. cit.*, p. 204 f.

62. Camara Laye, *The African Child*, Fontana Books, 6th impression, London, 1963, p. 103.

63. Colin Turnbull, *op. cit.*, p. 131 f.; cf. Mircea Eliade, *Birth and Rebirth*, New York, 1958, pp. 22–39.

64. Jomo Kenyatta, *op. cit.*, p. 148 ff.; Kenneth Little, *op. cit.*, p. 123.

65. Bruno Bettelheim, *Symbolic Wounds*, London, 1955, chapter on "Meaning of Initiation". Even Kenneth Little, who sees in the *Poro* Society among the Mende of Sierra Leone "common bonds" which unite fellow-members of the society over a wide area, seems to have only been able to detect the individual aspect of the initiatory rites (cf. *The Mende of Sierra Leone*, pp. 118–39).

66. Cf. Camara Laye, *op. cit.*, p. 104.

67. R. K. Yerkes, *op. cit.*, p. 49. We would here recall Bleeker's comment that "Each initiation is, in some respect, an unmasking" (Dr. C. J. Bleeker (ed.), *Initiation*, Leiden, 1965, p. 20).

68. Bernhard W. Anderson, *The Living World of the Old Testament*, new impression, London, 1961, p. 388.

69. Roy A. Stewart, *Rabbinic Theology*, London, 1961, p. 146 f.

M

Chapter 4

1. F. L. Cross, *St. Cyril of Jerusalem's Lectures on the Christian Sacraments*, London, 1951, *Procatechesis*, Cap. 5, p. 43.

2. *Ibidem*, Cap. 12, p. 48.

3. *Ibidem*, Cap. 13, p. 48.

4. Anglo–Catholic Prayer Book, London, p. 355, cf. Roman Missal *ad loc.*

5. *Christianity and African Culture*, A United Christian Gold Coast Publication, Accra, 1955, p. 60; cf. R. S. Rattray, *Ashanti*, p. 137 ff.; P. Amaury Talbot, *Tribes of Southern Nigeria*, Vol. II, p. 264.

6. C. H. Dodd, *New Testament Studies*, Manchester, 1953, p. 158; see also pp. 154–59.

7. S. Hofstra, the late Dutch anthropologist, quotes a Mende saying: "If I die, it cannot be helped. I am not going the way of a stranger. I shall meet my family there" (*Internationales Archiv fur Ethnographie*, Leiden, Band 39, 1941, p. 196).

8. L. S. Thornton, *Christ and the Church*, p. 135.

9. Jomo Kenyatta, *op. cit.*, p. 276 f.

10. *A Christian Year Book*, 1943 edition, London, p. 135; A. E. Southon, *Gold Coast Methodism*, London, 1953 (?), p. 24.

11. Cf. *Christianity and African Culture*, p. 6; Daryll Forde, *African Worlds*, p. 191; K. A. Busia, *Report on social survey of Sekondi-Takoradi*, London, 1950, pp. 79, 117.

12. *Christianity and African Culture*, p. 56.

13. Cf. K. A. Busia in Daryll Forde, *African Worlds*, p. 191.

14. C. G. Baeta, *Prophetism in Ghana*, London, 1962, pp. 20, 25, 39, 44, 69, 72, 92.

15. *Ibidem*, pp. 18, 54, 70, 133.

16. *Ibidem*, pp. 43, 48, 68.

17. *Ibidem*, pp. 43, 48, 68.

18. *Ibidem*, pp. 61, 142 f.; for parallel attitudes in South Africa, see Bengt Sundkler, *Bantu Prophets*, pp. 275–89; Dr. Idowu also describes a Nigerian Yoruba religious movement called *Orunmilaism* which is pagan in outlook with a liturgy "directed to *Olodumare* through *Orunmila*", based on a "Christian pattern" (*op. cit.*, p. 214).

19. K. A. Busia, *The Position of the Chief*, pp. 133–38, cf. Appendix III.

20. *The Church in Changing Africa*, Report of the All Africa Conference of Churches, Ibadan, 1955, p. 64 f.; cf. Mia Brandel-Syrier, *Black Woman in Search of God*, London, 1962, p. 149 f.

21. K. A. Busia in Daryll Forde, *African Worlds*, p. 208.

22. J. B. Danquah, *op. cit.*, p. 121.

23. J. F. Bethune Baker, *An Introduction to the Early History of Christian Doctrine*, 6th ed., London, 1938, p. 100 f.

24. J. B. Danquah, *op. cit.*, pp. 124, 127. Eva Meyerowitz, *The Divine Kingship in Ghana and Ancient Egypt*, p. 86 f.; *The Akan of Ghana*, p. 86 ff.

25. Mia Brandel-Syrier, *op. cit.*, p. 149. Miss Brandel-Syrier observes that "Christian Doctrine and Theology have not been able to replace the older systems of belief. . . . The status of Jesus amongst the ancestors and other spirits is not clear. . . . Jesus appears to have been fully accepted by the women (of Johannesburg) as an intermediary between man and God, and in this relationship God has sometimes been as shadowy, ill-defined and neutral as the tribal concept of the supreme Being." Later, she remarks, "There is no doubt that Jesus as the spiritual ancestor of man, as the ancestor of re-born man, would have been fully accepted and understood by the women" (p. 150).

26. H. Wheeler Robinson, *Redemption and Revelation*, London, 1947, p. 300 f.; cf. Cap. XIV, para. 3.

27. C. H. Dodd, *New Testament Studies*, p. 158.

28. E. B. Idowu, *op. cit.*, p. 197.

29. Eva Meyerowitz, *The Divine Kingship in Ghana and Ancient Egypt*, p. 121.

30. Ethelbert Stauffer, *op. cit.*, p. 212.

31. See *Book of Common Prayer 1662, Order for the Visitation of the Sick* (A Commendatory Prayer for a sick person at the point of departure).

32. Martensen, *Christian Dogmatics*, p. 457, quoted in *The Commemoration of Saints and Heroes of the Faith in the Anglican Communion*, London, 1958, p. 10; cf. Oscar Cullmann, *The Early Church*, ed. Higgins, London, 1957, Essay VII, and *Immortality of the Soul or Resurrection of the Dead*, London, 1958.

33. J. B. Danquah, *op. cit.*, p. 111.

34. Cf. E. Stauffer, *op. cit.*, Cap. 57; J. A. T. Robinson, *In the End God*, London, 1950.

35. See B. F. Westcott, *Ephesians*, London, 1906; Frank Weston, *The Revelation of Eternal Love*, London, 1920; Eric Mascall, *Christian Theology and Modern Science*, London, 1956; Norman Pittenger, *The Word Incarnate*, New York, 1959.

36. See J. H. Bernard, *St. John*, I.C.C., Edinburgh, 1942, p. cxvii. Cf. David Daube, *op. cit.*, Part III, Cap. IX.

37. Samuel Johnson, *A History of the Yorubas*, London, 1921, p. 38; E. B. Idowu, *op. cit.*, p. 68. See also p. 22.

38. R. S. Rattray, *Ashanti*, pp. 54, 146, 199; Daryll Forde, *African Worlds*, p. 193, essay by K. A. Busia.

39. Quoted by the Bishop of Chichester, *Christianity and World Order*, Penguin Books, London, 1940, p. 87.

Chapter 5

1. Cf. Margaret Field, *Religion and Medicine of the Ga People*, Accra and London, 1961 edition, Cap. III–IX; J. H. Nketia, *Music in Ghana*, Accra, 1962; E. B. Idowu, *op. cit.*, p. 113 ff.

2. *Christianity and African Culture*, p. 3; lecture by K. A. Busia on "The African World View".

3. Cf. Mircea Eliade, *Patterns in Comparative Religion*, p. 55; R. S. Rattray, *Ashanti*, p. 143 ff.; E. B. Idowu, *op. cit.*, Cap. 11; E. W. Smith, *African Ideas of God*, p. 52 f.; J. O. Lucas, *The Religion of the Yorubas*, Lagos, 1948, p. 248; *Présence Africaine*, July, 1958, p. 87, where William Leo Hansberry quoting from G. M. Theal, *Records of South-eastern Africa*, London, 1899, cites Damiago de Goes as saying that the Kaffirs ". . . believe in one God, the Creator of all things, and whom they adore and to whom they pray".

4. Cf. E. B. Idowu, *op. cit.*, pp. 75–79, 85–89; 214. See also p. 70.

5. *Christianity and African Culture*, p. 17. Cf. Harry Sawyerr, "Traditional Sacrificial Rituals and Christian Worship" in *Sierra Leone Bulletin of Religion*, Vol. II, No. 1, June 1960. For a discussion of *Two Sacrificial Rites in Sierra Leone*, see also the article by Harry Sawyerr in *Sierra Leone Bulletin of Religion*, No. I, June 1959; *Frontier*, Vol. 7, Spring 1964, article on "Sin and Forgiveness in Africa", by Harry Sawyerr. Dr. Meyer Fortes however suggests that "an ancestor is a named forbear who has living descendants of a designated genealogical class representing his continued structural relevance" (M. Fortes and G. D. Dieterlen, *African Systems of Thought*, London, 1965, p. 124; essay on "Some Reflections on Ancestor Worship"). But Fortes' suggestion does not fit into the Mende system, for example, where the forgotten names of revered dead are referred to as *Nde Blaa*. At the same time, an old unmarried man, and therefore one who has had no children, is regarded by the Lugbara as "unfit to offer sacrifice to the ancestors". After his death, he would soon be forgotten as a result (John Middleton, *Lugbara Religion*, London, 1960, p. 216).

6. Cf. *Christianity and African Culture*, p. 19, lecture by K. A. Busia on "Ancestor Worship, Libation, Stools Festivals".

7. W. Robertson Smith, *The Religion of the Semites*, revised ed., London, 1894, Lecture IX; cf. also E. B. Idowu, *op. cit.*, p. 122, on the Ɛbɔ Myth. Fela Sowande on the other hand has a different story, see *IFA*, p. 44 f.

8. E. B. Idowu, *op. cit.*, p. 192.

9. Edwin Smith, *op. cit.*, p. 25 footnote.

10. Jomo Kenyatta, *op. cit.*, p. 260 f.; but see the whole of Cap. X.

11. *Ibidem*, p. 232.

12. *Ibidem*, p. 239.

13. *Ibidem*, p. 234 f.

14. *Ibidem*, p. 239.

15. Mrs. Monica Wilson, *Communal Rituals among the Nyakyusa*, London, 1959, p. 162.

16. Cf. *ibidem*, p. 5.

17. *Ibidem*, p. 74.

18. *Ibidem*, p. 77.

19. *Ibidem*, p. 165 *et passim*.

20. E. B. Idowu, *op. cit.*, p. 69.

21. Ulli Beier, *A Year of Sacred Festivals*, p. 26.

22. K. A. Busia, *The Position of the Chief in the Modern Political System of Ashanti*, p. 96.

23. R. S. Rattray, *Ashanti*, pp. 80, 120, 136; Eva Meyerowitz, *The Sacred State of the Akan*, p. 149; cf. J. B. Danquah, *op. cit.*, p. 28.

24. R. S. Rattray, *Ashanti*, p. 216.

25. *Ibidem*, p. 215, footnote 3.

26. K. A. Busia, *The Position of the Chief in the Modern Political System of Ashanti*, p. 31 f., cf. p. 29.

27. E. B. Idowu, *op. cit.*, p. 116.

28. Jomo Kenyatta, *op. cit.*, p. 239.

29. *Ibidem*, p. 236.

30. Cf. *ibidem*, p. 74.

31. *Ibidem*, p. 239.

32. E. Evans-Pritchard, *Neuer Religion*, p. 119.

33. *Ibidem*, p. 22.

34. *Ibidem*, p. 27.

35. E. B. Idowu, *op. cit.*, p. 193.

36. *Ibidem*, pp. 9, 210; cf. Margaret J. Field, *Religion and Medicine of the Ga People*, p. 112; *Search for Security*, p. 98 ff.

37. *Ibidem*, p. 116.

38. Cf. Jahnheinz Jahn, *Muntu*, E.T. London, 1961, p. 63; J. V. Taylor, *Primal Vision*, London, 1963, p. 84.

39. E. B. Idowu, *op. cit.*, p. 193; cf. G. Parrinder, *Religion in an African City*, London, 1953, p. 44.

40. Ulli Beier, *op. cit.*, p. 26 f.

41. Robin Horton, *The Gods as Guests*, a Nigerian Magazine Publication, Lagos, 1960, p. 31. Much of this elation is, however, attributable to a prior draught of alcohol taken before the performances begin.

42. I owe this information to the Rev. F. G. Falusi and Mr. T. F. Fabiyi, both Yoruba men; the former was till recently assistant priest in St. George's Cathedral, Freetown; the latter is a graduate in theology, and a former student of Fourah Bay College.

A similar point of view is expressed by Louis Bouyer in relation to the word *sacrifice*. Although Bouyer said, in 1956, that the "deepest meaning of the word 'sacrifice' *sacrum facere* is 'to make holy'" (*Life and Liturgy*, p. 161), he has since come round to the position that "Originally, *sacrum facere* certainly did not mean 'to make sacred' . . . but rather quite simply 'to do what is sacred' *in se ac per se*. For the ancient Latins, sacrifice was nothing more than the sacred act" (*Rite and Man*, London, 1963, 79 f.). One common factor seems to be noticeable in the Yoruba and Christian attitudes described here, viz., the problem of clarifying the relation between the sacred and the profane. Cf. Mircea Eliade, *Patterns in Comparative Religion*, p. 31. It might be useful to recall Ernst Cassirer's important statement that, "The sacrifice is the point not only at which the profane and the sacred touch, but at which they permeate one another indissolubly" (*The Philosophy of Symbolic Forms*, Vol. II, New Haven, 1960, reprint, p. 227).

43. Robin Horton, *op. cit.*, p. 49.

44. Lowther Clarke, *Liturgy and Worship*, London, 1950, p. 28.

45. Cf. C. H. Dodd, *Romans*, Moffatt's Commentary, London, 1932, p. 43, where "faith" for St. Paul is defined as "an act which is the negation of all activity, a moment of passivity out of which strength for action comes, because in it God acts" (Notes on Romans 1: 17).

46. *International Review of Missions*, Vol. XLVII, No. 187, p. 269, article by J. H. Nketia on "African Culture and Christian Worship".

47. *Ibidem*, p. 271.

48. *Ibidem*, p. 272.

49. Cf. Edwin Smith, *African Beliefs and Christian Faith*, London, 1943, Part I; H. Debrunner, *op. cit.*, Cap. II–IV, VII.

50. Cf. *African Education*, A Study of Educational Policy and Practice in British Tropical Africa, Oxford, 1953, pp. 44, 58 f., 67–71, 100 f. Sir Eric Ashby, *Investment in Education*, Lagos, Nigeria, 1960, Cap. II; *African Universities and Western Tradition*, London, 1964, p. 41.

51. Cf. Hans-Gerard Koch, *The Abolition of God*, London, 1963, imp. Cap. 5, 6, 7; Fred Hoyle, *The Nature of the Universe*, London, 1963 ed., imp. Cap. 5.

52. Cf. K. A. Busia in *Christianity and African Culture*, p. 6; Daryll Forde, *African Worlds*, London, 1955, p. 196; *East and West Review*, Vol. XIV, No. 4, October 1948, pp. 110–13, article by Harry Sawyerr on "The African Adventure".

53. *Christianity and African Culture*, p. 60; lecture by Dr. C. G. Baeta on "The Challenge of the Church, and the Message of the Church to African Culture".

54. *Ibidem*, p. 55.

55. Cope, Davies and Tytler, *An Experimental Liturgy*, London, 1958, p. 26.

56. *The Book of Common Prayer*, London, 1662; cf. *The Prayer of Consecration in the Service of Holy Communion*; Fernard Prat, *The Theology of St. Paul*, E.T., London, 1945, Vol. II, p. 267 f.

57. Cf. *The Book of Common Prayer*, The Prayer of Oblation; Yngve Brilioth, *Eucharistic Faith and Practice*, London, 1953, p. 282 f.; Louis Bouyer, *Life and Liturgy*, p. 161.

58. L. Duschesne, *Christian Worship; Its Origin and Evolution* (E.T.), 5th edn., London, 1949, p. 401.

59. *Ibidem*, p. 283; cf. Lowther Clarke, *op. cit.*, pp. 365–73.

60. Matthew Black, *A Palestinian Syriac Horologion*, London, 1954, p. 89.

61. P. Edwall, E. Hayman and W. D. Maxwell, *Ways of Worship*, London, 1951, p. 309, Essay on *Mariology*; cf. E. L. Mascall and H. S. Box, *The Blessed Virgin Mary*, London, 1963, Cap. VIII; cf. Cap. VII for an evangelical reappraisal.

62. F. Edwall, E. Hayman and W. D. Maxwell, *op. cit.*, p. 313.

63. *Ibidem*, p. 314.

64. *Ibidem*, p. 317 f. Elsewhere, Max Thurian says of the Eucharist, "It provides a powerful means of integrating the whole life of the believers and their brotherly charity with the eucharistic celebration itself. ... The Eucharist becomes a privileged means of expressing brotherly charity and of self-giving in spiritual sacrifice" (*Eucharistic Memorial*, Part 2, London, 1963, p. 18). Later, Max Thurian, referring

to the Eucharistic liturgy, states that "The recalling of the saints together with the proclamation of the good news is a sign of a continuity of the Church and of the faithfulness of God, and it is a theological necessity that faith in the unity of the Body of Christ and in the communion of saints may be maintained" (*op. cit.*, p. 23).

65. F. Edwall, E. Hayman and W. D. Maxwell, *op. cit.*, p. 319.

66. Cf. pp. 121–27.

67. Cf. *Internationales Archiv fur Ethnographie*, Leiden, Band 39, 1941, p. 179 f., article by S. Hofstra on "The Ancestral Spirits of the Mendi".

68. M. J. Field, *Religion and Medicine of the Ga People*, pp. 8, 112 f.; *Africa*, Vol. X, 1937, p. 308, article by Jomo Kenyatta on "Kikuyu Religion, Ancestor Worship and Sacrificial Practices".

69. Cf. G. B. Gray, *Sacrifice in the Old Testament*, Oxford, 1925, p. 394.

70. Gregory Dix, *The Shape of the Liturgy*, 1st ed., 3rd impression, London, 1947, p. 162.

71. *Ibidem*, p. 244.

72. *Ibidem*, p. 243.

73. *Ibidem*, p. 162; cf. Max Thurian's comment that "The Eucharistic Memorial is a recalling to us, a recalling by us to the Father and a recalling of the Son to the Father for us" (*Eucharistic Memorial*, Part 2, p. 35 f.).

74. J. R. Wilson-Haffenden, *op. cit.*, p. 295.

75. Cf. Notes 28–31.

76. *Journal of Theological Studies*, New Series, Vol. VI, Part 2, article by the Rev. (now Canon) Douglas Jones, on *ANAMNHΣIΣ* in the LXX and the interpretation of 1 Cor. 11:25; cf. Max Thurian, *op. cit.*, p. 84, note 1.

77. J. Oldknow and A. D. Crake, *The Priest's Book of Devotion*, revised edition, London, 1952, p. 419.

78. *Ibidem*, p. 399.

79. D. W. Gundry, *Religions*, London, 1958, p. 68; C. A. Campbell, *Selfhood and Godhood*, London, 1957, p. 202. Gundry's discussion of this aspect of the rites of the primitive religions leaves out of all consideration the salient comment made by Louis Bouyer that it is in the realm of magical practices that man attempts "to gain control over the divine and reduce it to one's mercy". On the other hand in religion, man "bows down before the presence of the divinity" (*Rite and Man*, p. 82). Ernst Cassirer also makes the poignant remark that "Fundamentally, every sacrifice implies a negative factor: a limitation of sensory desire, a renunciation which the I imposes on itself". And again, "The magical spell . . . exerts

an unlimited power over the gods, bending them and forcing their will, ... But in the very first stages of sacrifice we find a different trend of human will and action. For the power imputed to the sacrifice is rooted in the self-renunciation of sacrifice. ..." (*The Philosophy of Symbolic Forms*, New Haven, Vol. II, 1955, p. 221 f.)

80. D. Westermann, *Christianity and Africa*, London, 1937, p. 100; cf. M. J. Field, *Search for Security*, p. 88.

81. R. D. Yerkes, *Sacrifice in Greek and Roman Religions and in Early Judaism*, London, 1953, p. 20 f.

82. *Harvard Theological Review*, Vol. XLIV, No. 3, July 1957, p. 116.

83. *Classical Quarterly*, Vol. 32, Nos. 3, 4, p. 223, article by O. Skutch and H. J. Rose. Cf. also essay by A. G. Hebert, "A Root of Difference and Unity", in D. Baillie and J. Marsh, *Intercommunion*, London, 1952, pp. 241, 249.

84. Yngve Brilioth, *Eucharistic Faith and Practice*, p. 282.

85. *Ibidem*, p. 283 f.; cf., p. 69.

86. O. C. Quick, *The Christian Sacraments*, London, 1946, p. 194.

87. *Ibidem*, p. 194 f.; cf. L. S. Thornton, *The Common Life in the Body of Christ*, Cap. II, XIV; F. Prat, *op. cit.*, p. 351, where the author, quoting St. Chrysostom, stresses that in 1 Cor. 10: 16 f., "St. Paul does not say *participation*, but *communion*, because he wishes to express a closer union. For in receiving Communion, we not only participate in Christ, we unite with him."

88. F. N. Hicks in F. Edwall, E. Hayman and W. D. Maxwell, *op cit.*, p. 309; cf. Charles Gore, *The Body of Christ*, London, 1901, Cap. III.

89. Cf. Monica Wilson, *Communal Rituals of the Nyakyusa*, London, 1959, pp. 113, 114, 160 ff.

90. Anton Fridrischen, *The Root of the Vine*, London, 1953, p. 93. Essay by Harald Stahlin; cf. Louis Bouyer's comment that "... the element of 'Communion' means that the Eucharist is a meal, a community meal, in which all the participants are brought together to have a common share in common goods, these common goods being first of all the bread and wine of a real human meal, whatever their deeper significance" (*op. cit.*, p. 76, cf. p. 182 f.); cf. also E. O. James, *The Nature and Function of Priesthood*, London, 1955, p. 160; W. D. Davies, *Paul and Rabbinic Judaism*, London, 1948, p. 251.

91. G. B. Gray, *op. cit.*, p. 209.

92. F. Edwall, E. Hayman and W. D. Maxwell, *op. cit.*, p. 209.

93. St. Ignatius, *Ad Ephesianos*, Cap. 20: 2.

94. *Ibidem*, Cap. 13.

95. Canon J. V. Taylor has rightly suggested both "some form of 'open' confession within the fellowship, as well as private confession in the presence of a priest in order to satisfy the troubled conscience and reinstate the penitent" (*op. cit.*, p. 194).

96. Cf. *The Church's Ministry of Healing*, London, 1958, *imp.*, Cap. V–VII; J. V. Taylor, *op. cit.*, p. 152; Lewis Maclachlan, *Clergy-Doctor Cooperation*, London, 1964, Cap. V.

97. W. T. Kimber, *The Healing Church*, London, 1962, p. 96. Dr. Kimber makes two comments which are relevant to this discussion viz.: (*a*) that "From earliest pre-Christian times, the healer who treated any form of illness was both priest and physician" (p. 21); (*b*) that "The Church in advocating the practice of self-examination, confession and absolution, provides the means of achieving the wholeness of individuation. This is often a humbling, but certainly a cleansing experience which is the basis for obtaining grace for amendment of life—a rebirth" (p. 54).

98. Cf. L. Duschesne, *op. cit.*, Cap. VIII, *imp.*, p. 288; E. O. James, *Christian Myth and Ritual*, London, 1933, on valid and invalid "invocations of the saints"; cf. *The Commemoration of Saints and Heroes of the Faith in the Anglican Communion*, London, 1958, p. 12.

99. J. Danielou, *The Lord of History*, London, 1959, p. 121.

100. *The Commemoration of Saints and Heroes of the Faith in the Anglican Communion*, p. 50, *et passim*. Cf. E. M. Almedingen, *Dom Bernard Clements*, London, 1945, p. 82; W. G. de Lara Wilson, *Christianity and Native Rites*, London, 1950, p. 21.

101. Cf. E. O. James, *The Nature and Function of Priesthood*, p. 176; see the whole of Cap. VI. For a useful discussion of Christian Priesthood, see H. Balmforth, *Christian Priesthood*, London, 1963.

102. Cf. Edmund Morgan, *The Ordeal of Wonder*, London, 1964, p. 120; Dorothee Hoch, *Healing and Salvation*, London, 1958, pp. 34–41.

103. See Note 53 below.

104. E. B. Idowu, *op. cit.*, pp. 69, 202 f.

Epilogue

1. L. E. Elliott-Binns, *English Thought, 1860–1900*, London, 1956, p. 205.

2. *Ibidem*, p. 205, footnote.

3. Cf. *Survey of the Training of the Ministry in Africa, Part II*, London, 1954, Cap. III.

4. Cf. Bengt Sundkler, *The Christian Ministry in Africa*; F. G. Welch, *Training for the Ministry in East Africa*, Limuru, 1963, Part V, pp. 105–62.

5. W. G. de Lara Wilson, *op. cit.*, p. 48, essay by E. O. James; cf. Christopher Dawson's comment that "... the particular goods of particular cultures are not dead ends; they are the media by which the universal good is apprehended and through which these cultures are orientated towards the good that transcends their own power and knowledge" (*Religion and Culture*, London, 1949, p. 62); *Ministry, A Theological Review*, Morija, Basutoland, Vol. III, No. 4, July 1963, pp. 151–58, article by E. B. Idowu; E. B. Idowu, *Towards an Indigenous Church*, Ibadan and London, 1965. Adjai Crowther the great African pioneer missionary to Nigeria anticipated these writers when, in a charge delivered at Lokoja, Nigeria, on September 13, 1869, he said, *inter alia*, "... it should be borne in mind that Christianity does not undertake to destroy national assimilation: where there are many degrading and superstitious defects it corrects them; ..." Crowther's words still ring true today as arising out of a deep Christian insight into the needs for the true Christianization of Africa. For a fuller discussion of Crowther's position and its modern relevance see *International Review of Missions*, Vol. LIV, No. 215, July 1965, pp. 343–52, article by Harry Sawyerr on "Christian Evangelistic Strategy in West Africa"; cf. J. F. A. Ajayi, *Christian Missions in Nigeria 1841–1891*, London, 1965, pp. 216–32.

INDEX

Adae 101, 124, 154
Adwera 124, 154
Akan 18 f., 21, 48, 54, 65, 102–04, 109, 119, 124, 129
Ale, Ala 22
Allen, Roland 39, 63
Anamnesis, Christian 140 f., 146
    Mende 146 f.
Ancestors 12, 23, 26–28, 53, 90 f., 94, 96, 119, 122 ff., 132, 134, 138 f., 141, 142 f., 171, 172
Ancestor worship 54, 90, 97, 110 f., 119 f., 121–29, 135, 141
Apostolic succession (Pagan) 85
Asaase Afua 22
Asaase Yaa 22, 100 f.
Asamoa, E. 81
Asantehene 53, 85, 100
Ashanti Confederacy 22
Awujɔ 147, 197

Baeta, C. G. 96, 97, 132, 155
Bantu of Lower Congo 18
Beier, Ulli 123, 127 f.
Bettelheim, Bruno 89
Blood, life- 18, 121
    of circumcision 24, 87, 90
    -covenant 89 f., 121
Busia, K. A. 96, 100

Carrington, Archbishop Philip 35
Chameleon 17, 19
Chief 72 f.
Christian Church 79–81, 83
    the Great Family 71, 85 f., 91, 106
Christian life, Pauline teaching on, in I Thessalonians 37 f.
Clarke, Lowther 130
Clergy, future training of 64
Confessions, Christian 129, 153, 178
    Pagan 120–21, 155
Covenant, blood- 52, 89 f., 92, 121, 134

Hebrew 43, 51 f.
    -relationship 51–53, 86
    with the dead 52
Creation 13 f., 48
Creationism 23
Creole, Sierra Leone 19, 27 f., 125, 150

Davies, J. G. 133
Danquah, J. B. 102, 104
Dead, deification of 54
    covenant with 52, 95
    food for 150
Death 17 f., 48
Debrunner, H. 78 f.
Denney, James 60
Destiny 20
Divination 97–100, 122, 127 f.
Dodd, C. H. 95
Double, man's 20, 21

Earth 23, 25
    goddess 21, 22
    Mother- 22, 23, 24, 25 f.
    Nzambi 25
    a power 22 f., 24
Eclipses of sun and moon 17
Eucharist 10, 38, 144–50, 153, 175, 177
Evil 17, 20
    and destiny 20
    and world-order 21
    sources of 21
    a diminution of power-force 21

Field, Margaret 15, 70, 78, 139
Fueter, Paul de 72

God, names of:
    Kurumasaba 29
    Kyala 123
    Leve 34
    Leza 25

Mwene Nyaga 16, 124 f., 141
Ngai 119, 122 f., 125 f.
Nyankopon 53, 65, 109
Nzambi 22, 25
Ɗgewɔ 25, 65
Odomankoma 65
Olodumare 45, 48, 49 f., 79, 119
Olofin-Orun 165
Ɔbrun 65
Onyame, Nyame 29, 65
Uwoluwu 49
Yataa 29
God, and creation 14 ff., 44–51, 65,
    112, 132, 146
  covenant-making 51
  the Father of the deities 14, 33,
    44–49, 68, 115
  the source of all life 13, 34
  the source of good and evil 21,
    116 f.
  and Nature 16, 115, 130
  the Great Ancestor 29
  Hebrew concept of 50–53
  man's Protector 15, 73, 100
  and sin, in the African situation
    15, 32
  omnipotence of 112–17
  otherness of 49, 51
  passibility of 116
  Supreme Being 13, 115
  permissive will of 14, 115
  punishing sin 15 f.

Hodgson, Leonard 79
Hɔmɔwa 154
Holland, H. S. 33
Holy Spirit 37 f., 59, 106, 111, 154 f.
homoousion 68
Horton, Robin 128
Howells, A. W. 83

Ibo 22
Idowu, E. B. 20, 46 f., 48 f., 52,
    79, 119, 121, 123, 127, 155
Illness (see Sickness)
Initiation rites 85 f.
  a rebirth 87–89, 93

Jakuta 49

Jesus Christ, Paul on, in 1 Thessa-
    lonians 35
  Agent of Creation 74
  Founder of the Great Family, the
    Church 79
  Incarnation of 72–91, 103–107,
    111, 113–17, 133
  Son of God 73–9

Kenyatta, Jomo 88, 122, 125 f.
Kikuyu 16, 19, 25, 86, 88, 96, 124 f.,
    141
Kimber, W. J. T. 153, 178
Kingship, divine 53 f., 65
Kinship, age-mate 85–90, 92
Kono 19, 32
Kposso 49
Kra 53, 109
Kroo of Liberia 23, 28
Kwotto 21, 141

La Kpa 71
Laye, Camara 87
Leenhardt, F. J. 61
Libations 101 f., 124
Liturgy, shape of pagan 120 f.
  probable shape of a Christian,
    for Africa 151–52

Maa Ndɔɔ 22
Maa Ɗgewɔ 22
Malinke 86 f.
Martensen 110
Mary, a black 81
Memento Domine 10, 93
Mende 10, 14, 18, 21, 29, 34, 44,
    65, 84, 89, 91, 104, 125, 169,
    170, 172
Messiah, Akan 102–05
Meyerowitz, Eva 18, 22
Monogamy 81–83

Nana 53 f., 102–04, 106
Nature 16, 75
Nicene Creed 68
Nicholls, W. 68 f.
Nketia, J. H. 101, 132
Ntorɔ 71, 105
Nyakyusa 123

Oduduwa 53, 123
Oni of Ife 53
Opanyim 54, 102–04, 106
Ori (see Destiny)
Orisa-nla 45, 46, 48, 54, 75
Orisha, She 127–28
Orogi 5, 107
Orunmila 20, 74, 170

Parrinder, G. 82, 84
Phillips, G. 40, 64
Polygamy 81–83
  in Old Testament 42
Poro 23, 31, 125, 169
Presence 26 ff.
  of cultic spirits 28
  of the dead 26, 28
  of God 29, 129, 133
Priest, Christian 154
  cultic 137–39, 153, 155
  -kings 53, 54, 85, 119, 141
Priestcraft 157
Pritchard, E. Evans- 126

Ramsey, Lisle 82
Rattray, R. S. 84, 124
Rice, red-palm-oil 91
Robinson, Wheeler 109

Sacrifice 11, 38, 101, 119 ff.,
  122–28, 132–46, 174, 176
  Christian 38, 140–51
Saints, worship of 134
Sango 123
Sensus Communis 30 f.
Sexual intercourse, prohibition of
  21, 25, 143
Shigidi 28
Sickness and death 17 f., 48, 116,
  148
Sin 15, 30–32
  and guilt 30 f.
  and sickness 30, 138
Solidarity of community 12, 30 f.,
  138
  of family 122, 125 f., 147
  in Old Testament 43

Sopona 49
Sowande, Fela 47 f.
Spirits, ancestral (see Ancestors)
  cultic 132, 142 f.
  evil 19
  worship of 7, 76, 120
Squire, Sir John 117
Sropa 49
Suffering, Christian attitude to 117,
  133
  pagan attitude 116, 133
Sundkler, B. 13, 41, 84, 157
Sunsum 105

Talbot, P. Amaury 21
Tano 115
Taylor, J. V. 26, 82, 178, 182
Testament, Old 33 f., 39–43, 53,
  55, 58, 60 f., 112 f.
  New 64, 81, 113
Temne 18, 21, 44, 54, 125
Tempels, Fr. P. 78 f.
Thurian, Max 136 f.
Trowell, Margaret 83 f.
Turnbull, Colin 86 f.

Urbanization 131

Wand, J. W. C. 80
Watu wa Mngu 96
Westermann, D. 142
Wilson, Monica 123
Witch-cloak 19, 24
Witchcraft 17, 19, 107, 131 f.
  and sickness 32
  destruction of 107
  in Old Testament 42
  Orogi 107
Woman, menstrual 18, 21
  pregnant 17, 19
Worship, Christian 129 f.
  cultic 120, 127, 137, 152
  transformation of African, for
  Christ 130

Yerkes, R. D. 143
Yoruba 19 f., 22, 44, 65, 84, 109,
  115, 121, 123 f., 127